The
SEA
NEVER
CHANGES

~~~~~~~~~~~~~~~

My Singlehanded

The SEA

Trimaran Race
Around the World

NEVER CHANGES

OLIVIER de KERSAUSON
with Christian Bex

Translated and with a Foreword
by Alison Anderson

SHERIDAN HOUSE

First published 1992 by
Sheridan House Inc.
145 Palisade Street
Dobbs Ferry, NY 10522

Copyright © Flammarion 1990
English translation © Sheridan House 1992

First published in France under the title
Vieil Océan by
Flammarion

Design by Jeremiah B. Lighter
Map by Eric W. Sponberg
Cover photo by Christophe Mahé
Photos inside by Christian Février, except
Photo at Mar del Plata by I. Bich/Sygma

Library of Congress Cataloging-in-Publication Data

Kersauson, Olivier de.
    [Vieil océan. English]
    The sea never changes / Olivier de Kersauson ; as with Christian Bex ;
translated by Alison Anderson.
        p.   cm.
    Translation of: Vieil océan.
    ISBN 0-924486-22-8 : $17.95
    1. Yacht racing. 2. Poulain (Trimaran) 3. Sailing, Single-handed.
    4. Kersauson, Olivier de. I. Bex, Christian. II. Title.
GV832.K4813   1992
797.1'4—dc20   92-6
                                                                CIP

ISBN 0-924486-22-8
Printed in the United States of America

ACKNOWLEDGEMENTS

France Info

TF1

Thalassa, FR3

Claude Fons

The City of Brest

The Port of Brest

The French Navy

The Club Nautico of
Mar del Plata

SARSAT

ARGOS

Marc Menaud

Jean-Michel and Annie
Texier - "Le Pré-Vert"

———— ✳ *v* ✳ ————

OLIVIER de KERSAUSON's

Record Solo Circum-navigation

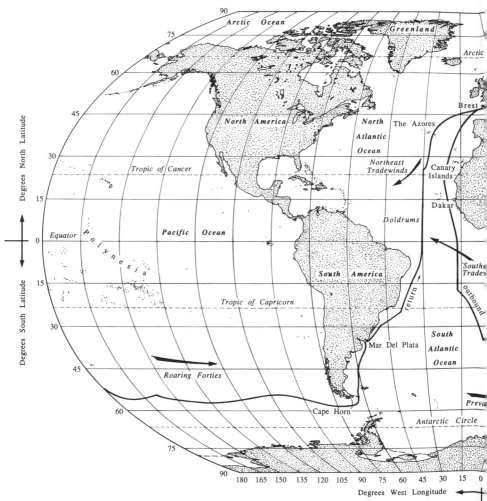

Map prepared by Eric W. Sponberg, naval architect
Sponberg Yacht Design Inc.
Newport, Rhode Island
February 1992

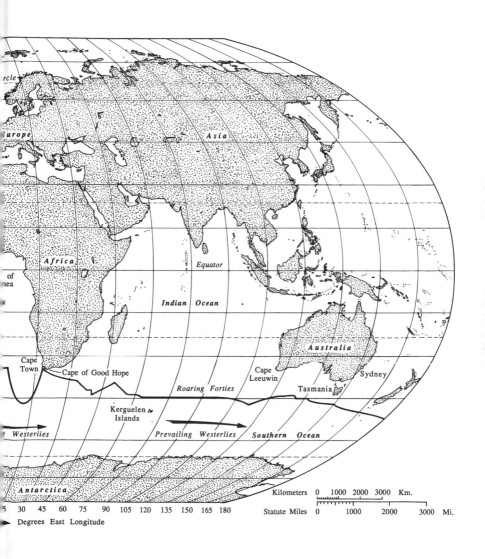

Europe

Asia

Africa

Equator

Indian Ocean

Australia

Cape Town

Cape of Good Hope

Cape Leeuwin

Sydney

Roaring Forties

Tasmania

Kerguelen Islands

Westerlies

Prevailing Westerlies

Southern Ocean

Antarctica

Kilometers 0 1000 2000 3000 Km.

Statute Miles 0   1000   2000   3000 Mi.

5   30   45   60   75   90   105 120 135 150 165 180

Degrees East Longitude

FOREWORD

IN RECENT YEARS an impressive number of sailing records and trophies have been captured by men and women from France. Where there is a race or a challenge there are French sailors—particularly when the race is a singlehanded circumnavigation. Then there are those who set out alone—like Olivier de Kersauson—with no fleet of competitors reassuringly nearby, to try for a new record: after twenty years of ocean racing, the solo, non-stop circumnavigation is a logical challenge, and a ripe opportunity to test the speed and endurance of the multihull, grown so popular in France for offshore racing.

In 1975, a friend and compatriot of Kersauson's, Alain Colas, was the first to beat Sir Francis Chichester's solo circumnavigation record, on his multihull *Manureva.* Colas' record of 169 days, with stops, stood for 13 years until Philippe Monnet, on his trimaran *Kriter Brut de Brut,* sliced 40 days off Colas' record. So a greater challenge awaited Olivier de Kersauson when he set sail only a year later to try to beat Monnet's record, hoping to make it a non-stop circumnavigation. He would carve another four days off Monnet's time and hold the record for a year until yet another Frenchman, Titouan Lamazou, won the Vendée Globe Challenge in 1990 on a monohull with a non-stop time of 109 days. The first- and second-place winners of the 1990-91 BOC Challenge, Christophe Auguin and Alain Gautier, completed the course in 120 and 122 days respectively—with all the support granted to racers in a competition of this kind, and the time to recoup after each leg. Kersauson still holds the record for a solo circumnavigation on a multihull—a considerably more dangerous and demanding feat than a monohull circumnavigation.[1]

In France, Kersauson, Monnet, Lamazou and Florence Arthaud are household names. Ocean racing and circumnavigations are followed by the media and the general public with a passion given in the United States

---

1. Other records set by Kersauson: fastest crossing of the Indian Ocean (7590 miles at 10.2 knots); fastest crossing of the South Pacific (5340 miles at 10.52 knots); fastest crossing between the Cape of Good Hope and Cape Horn (13,020 miles at 10.3 knots); and the fastest 7-day passage (2361 miles at 12.268 knots, average speed, south of Australia).

only to major league baseball or football. The brilliance of the French performance in sailing may have two explanations: first, almost all skippers receive considerable financial aid from corporate sponsors, and their boats are named after banks, dairy products, champagnes... But the second, perhaps more significant explanation for their success may lie within the national character itself: fiercely independent and individualistic, the French often prefer solitude to teamwork, and excel at doing things alone, their own way. Long before technology gave birth to the current high-profile generation of speed sailors, solo circumnavigators like Jean Cau or Bernard Moitessier were quietly leaving the ports of Brest or La Rochelle and sailing around the world for years.

Kersauson's account of this 125-day circumnavigation is evidence of that same spirit of independence; moreover, like Moitessier, he displays a love of nature and a sense of philosophical inquiry which transcend mere love of the sport or the desire for fame or fortune.

Alison Anderson
Sausalito, December 1991

*"The sea never changes
and its works, for all the talk of men,
are wrapped in mystery."*

Joseph Conrad,
Typhoon

1

I DIDN'T KNOW—and wouldn't find out until after my return—that I had crossed the starting line between the Petit Minou lighthouse and the Fillettes buoy at exactly 11:52 A.M. Eleven fifty-two on December 28, 1988! I knew that I must be crossing the line just at that moment, but it was not something I could see. Nor did I check the stopwatch; I left that chore to my crew on the launch which had followed me out of the harbor.

We had all been preparing for my departure since seven o'clock that morning. On the ground floor of a large house facing the harbor was my office-cum-storeroom. Surrounded by my crew in the midst of a clutter of rope and cardboard boxes, I had reviewed mentally the list of the gear on board, the list of provisions...

The collar of my jacket turned up for warmth, I tried to concentrate in the raw light of the two bare bulbs which pierced the December night. Everyone respected the silence where I'd already shut myself away. I waited until it was actually light out before leaving my den; at around nine I walked down to the docks...my last steps on land. A handful of friends came to say goodbye— ten or so, not more; an intimate farewell, no outbursts. Throats were tight but everyone contained their emotion, out of modesty. Perhaps, also, not to upset me with their anxiety. Then I called out the orders to set us free: "Cast off bow lines! Cast off astern!" The boat pulled away from the dock and began her slow descent along the channel. For four months, the boat would be my entire universe.

I went out on the tide, and the weather was almost fine. The sea was lumpy, the sky filled with torn clouds through which pale sunbeams shone, lighting now the sea, now the boat, like a searchlight. My big pink trimaran pulled away, waddling on her floats like a duck.

The maneuver to leave the harbor went very smoothly and I realized I was truly on my way only when Caroline, my wife, and Arthur, my son, were no more than waving silhouettes on the launch. Arthur was wearing one of my windbreakers; I could tell he was cold. And then the next step: the crew-members who had helped me out of the harbor now left the boat. When Yves and Didier left I knew, by the looks we exchanged, the farewell kisses, that I was on my own—I was on my way. But that was no surprise; what I was experiencing at that moment was merely the continuation of an ongoing process, begun long before.

In fact I had been gone for two and a half months already, a time during which my life had been turned on its ear—taking meals at certain times, sleeping at certain times, getting up in the middle of the night to ride my bike or lift weights. Two and a half months with nothing else on my mind but this circumnavigation. It had already become such an obsession that long before my actual departure I had virtually no contact with my surroundings. The only time I came back to earth during that time was to deal with last-minute financial or technical problems. In every other aspect I was already locked away in the program which would allow me to complete my circumnavigation as quickly as possible.

I had gone over the route step by step before my departure, perhaps ten, twenty times. While riding my bike near Brest I would envision the course, going over it in the light of everything I knew about the sea, all my memories, and all I could imagine about how the boat we had fitted out would behave. So for two and a half months I had not been able to communicate with others. I had already left, I was completely cut off from everything.

When you leave to sail around the world you leave for so long that there is no real time or place you can qualify as a starting point. It's not like a hundred-yard dash. You're committing yourself to such an adventure that you have to put a lot of your life into it—particularly as you're not sure whether you'll return. And that is why I felt no wrenching emotion when I crossed the line. I was hardly aware of it.

The only true emotion came when I realized I hadn't had time to say goodbye to Arthur as I would have liked. Shortly before I cast off he had come on board. He had played around with the rigging but his expression had been serious and he was silent. That was the first fright of my trip. I said to myself that this child must not grow up without me. Would life look after him as he should be looked after? He was only eight, so it was unlikely. And so I understood that I *had* to come back—it was imperative—to look after him. We exchanged a few words but it was a train-station sort of farewell, immediately swept away by the wind. I spoke to him about school, I pleaded with him to work hard while I was away, to make an effort. Then I tried to reassure him, because I thought I could read fear in his eyes, and that I did not want. But in my mind I had already left and no one, not even my family, was living on the same emotional plane as I was.

All the meaningful projects of my life have been carried out in solitude, and I knew that once again solitude was waiting for me. I would have to travel full circle— down past the Canary Islands, off the African coast past Dakar, cut across the equator, leave the Cape of Good Hope to port, pass the Kerguelen Islands, sail south of Tasmania, set a southward course to Cape Horn, then up through the Atlantic and back to Brest— before I would be back on the same plane as Arthur.

In fact I'd been gone for a very long time. Not just two or three months, but easily three, five years, maybe more. Solo circumnavigation is every sailor's ultimate dream. It's the project which has always given me, in any case, the greatest motivation. I had already been around the world twice on crewed boats, the first time in 1973 as Eric Tabarly's first mate,[1] the second time as skipper of *Kriter II*.[2] And now I felt that *Poulain*,[3] my boat, as the progenitor of a new generation of multihulls, had, sooner or later, to embark on the strongest, the richest, the most complex adventure to be had at sea. What with the distance, the risk, flat calm or storm, a circumnavigation has everything to offer, and I felt it was time to see what a boat of this type was capable of, if for no other reason than the fact that multihulls have been around for twenty years. That's more than a coming of age, it's a generation. Twenty years ago Tabarly, Alain Colas, myself, and a few others set off on the ocean with the first multihulls. We didn't know at the time where these boats could take us. They've had ample opportunity since then to prove their endurance and competitiveness. Multihulls account for the greatest changes in yachting over the past two decades. There have been countless new inventions and records broken, between *Pen-Duick IV*,[4] the first multihull worthy of the name, and today's fleet; there have been discoveries, thousands upon thousands of miles under the hulls; there have been accidents, breakdowns, deaths as well, and, at the same time, true progress.

Poulain was not just any multihull, she was a trimaran. Trimarans are the best

1. During the first Whitbread race. (T.N.)
2. Financial Times Clipper Race, 1975-76, won by *Great Britain II*. (T.N.)
3. At the time of Kersauson's circumnavigation, his trimaran sailed—and is often listed—under the name of *Un Autre Regard*. The name was changed for sponsorship reasons.
4. Eric Tabarly's first record-making trimaran, later owned by Alain Colas. (T.N.)

multihulls for the sea; their axis of capsize runs through the central hull, a promise of greater stability than on a catamaran. I haven't had much experience on catamarans, but I do know that over the last five years the world fleet of multihulls has come to be made up of an overwhelming majority of trimarans. What remains to be shown is that they are also capable of a circumnavigation at breakneck speed—even if the risk involved is much greater. While a monohull will right itself after being knocked down, a trimaran, once it has flipped over, cannot right itself on the open sea. It's as good as lost.

For any boat a circumnavigation is the equivalent of the Kentucky Derby for a racehorse; those which succeed in this ultimate test will have the greatest chance for posterity. *Poulain* was created in the spirit of round-the-world racing. She had taken part in other races, which was gratifying in itself, but she was conceived with a circumnavigation in mind, and not just any circumnavigation—a non-stop circumnavigation.

And so as I crossed the line on that

December morning, the 28th, at 11:52, I felt, for a number of reasons, that I had already been circumnavigating for three years at least, from the time *Poulain* was conceived in 1985.

2

A T THE TIME of my departure the weather was rather nice. I was wearing a thin sweater and the winds were light. Even though these were not the conditions I'd dreamt of for departure, I still felt that the event had gone as smoothly as could be expected, and deep down I was fairly content.

For three weeks I'd been waiting for the weather to be on my side; for three weeks I'd been calling my weather router, Claude Fons, director of the National Weather Bureau in Brest. A tall man with a thin moustache and greying temples, always very precise in his choice of words, he described to me, day after day, with a trace of an accent from the south, a completely abnormal anticyclone over a large part of the Atlantic, with winds from the south all along the coast of Africa—straight on the nose. I lived through those three weeks under unbearable tension, waiting without respite for the green light to set sail.

I'd invested everything in this circumnavigation—I'd even had to sell my house in La Trinité to keep my family from financial worry. I'd worked like a galley slave to get all the gear I needed and I'd worn my nerves too thin to decide to delay my departure for another year.

The decision to leave in December was based on nautical common sense: I needed to be able to sail through the south in the most favorable, least impossible conditions for this type of boat. I absolutely had to take advantage of the southern summer, and so I had no other choice than to leave France at the beginning of winter. Even so, the southern summer is no tropical paradise. At the same latitude it is much colder in the south and at latitude 52-53° snow is not unusual. Imagine snow in Cherbourg in the middle of August!

During the day on December 27 the

anticyclone finally began to move off, making the conditions for departure acceptable. If I'd had better conditions earlier I might not have been able to take advantage of them anyway, as my sails and part of my equipment were not delivered until December 20.

At least we could go over everything one last time. My land crew made thorough inspections and preparations—I was not about to set off on this adventure filled with risk, as is any adventure, without having done my utmost to have luck on my side and to ensure that I had a "good crate" under me.

A sailboat which is about to circumnavigate is not made ready in the same way as a centerboard dinghy on the way out for a jaunt on a pond. Everything is prepared with one thing in mind: to sail the entire loop without one single stop. *Poulain* had been set up to be totally self-sufficient for the four months or so that the journey would take. Every single piece of gear had been thoroughly inspected according to the technical and financial standards we could afford. And since we were not exactly NASA, we had to put our trust in the specifications and guarantees offered by the suppliers. We were never able to make any full, real-life tests. Some of the gear on board had been tested, but for a different use than that which we were going to make of it. Every boat is an experiment and *Poulain* was no exception, so it was up to us whether to trust our suppliers or not: we had to try to sense how truthful, reliable, or incompetent they were. It was a real puzzle.

A sailboat of the size and complexity of *Poulain* can account for 2500 invoices. Every invoice corresponds to equipment loaded on board and must therefore be preceded by careful reflection. Months of ant-like work are required: reinforce the halyards, avoid stress points, go over the central hull with a fine-tooth comb, examine all the vents and through-hulls, the advantages of keeping them or maintaining them... Then we had to inspect all the standing and running rigging, all the deck fixtures, and make a thorough study of the electrical system to find how best to obtain a good current without putting the navigational instruments at risk from a drop in voltage. We finally opted for a half-way solution: produce direct current and send it to the instruments on two separate circuits for added protection. We had to resort to similar technical acrobatics regarding the storage of fuel for the generator. By the end of the journey the tank would be nearly empty; but how would the gradual reduction in the fuel weight affect the boat's trim as the journey progressed—and for that matter, should we not distribute all the food and consumable stores in ways that would best conform to the sea states we anticipated on the journey? And so on. Everything brought on board was examined, inspected, weighed.

And yet there is no such thing as a "special circumnavigation" boat. A stock round-the-world boat does not exist. A boat is simply designed according to certain criteria which must enable it to go round the world. It's simple logic: a solid body, capable of standing up to the elements, capable of making the effort and going the extra mile, and capable of making an Olympic-class sprint as well, for speed is essential. Nor must the boat be too heavy.

This is what we tried to achieve with *Poulain*. As she had already been sailed quite a lot and shown what she was capable of (second in the Course de l'Europe,[5] although she was the only boat with an aluminum mast in the competition), a large number of the problems had already been eliminated. But we still had to anticipate the sort of risks we would be taking on what we wanted to be a non-stop course.

We had to think about the shape and size of the mast that would be best adapted to the course. On a multihull each additional pound aloft acts like a colossal lever when the boat rolls, and can lead to a capsize. I finally chose a carbon fiber mast, which was delivered almost at the last moment to replace the aluminum one I'd had at the time of the Course de l'Europe. With carbon fiber, a composite material, I was saving 700 pounds! Of the boat's total weight of nearly nine and a half tons, 1800 pounds were rigging alone, nearly ten per cent. That sounded a good percentage, but how could I be sure?

Sailing, despite all the technology one

5. Round-Europe Race.

carries on board, despite studies in laboratories, is still a matter of guesswork. We are sure of nothing! And we'll never be sure of a thing as long as we have no precise measuring instruments. Aviation engineers are beginning to understand what's going on because they do have the instruments—colossal sums of money have been spent just on ways to measure the effects of their experiments. Manufacturers have the luxury of losing one, two, or three planes during the initial tests for each new aircraft model. Same thing in the auto industry: when Renault brings out a variation of the R5, their research department will have spent enormous amounts just to study the shape of the radiator grill! But for us poor sailors each boat is a prototype which may have some offspring, but never an assembly-line posterity, and we are condemned to constant trial-and-error. We may think we're making better use of science, but all that's happened is that the range of our ignorance has been reduced. We have information and experience, no doubt of that, but we're nowhere near true knowledge. All we can do is anticipate the risks. That's not much, but it's not negligible either. When I set off around the globe, I knew it was a poor man's job.

In a way I might reasonably claim that at the moment I slipped my mooring, ninety per cent of the work had already been done. The majority of the potential hazards had already been forestalled. Departure was nothing more or less than the practical realization of all the ideas revolving around the boat, of two or three years of saying to ourselves, "Okay, we're going to do it!"

And now we had to prove that we were right to do it.

3

THE LAND DISAPPEARED very quickly. As we left Brest I watched the outline of the town—the channel, the coast; I watched the headlands, but very soon I could no longer make anything out. In any case the point was not to view the landscape; that no longer interested me. I was away, I was very happy, and that was all that mattered. So I lit up a cigarette, brewed a little cup of decaf, and began to tidy up below.

Poulain was a superb beast. A long trimaran—75 feet in length with a beam of 52 feet; a mast 82 feet high and a mainsail measuring 1600 square feet. A good-looking boat with a real gift for the sea. I had already put some 20,000 miles under her keel so I knew precisely how she would react and also how she was propelled by her rigging, mast, and sails. I knew I had a remarkable boat beneath my feet; one which had, moreover, been set up for a man alone, with the best possible use of space. It would not be too tight a squeeze because I had a space of roughly 86 square feet. 86 square feet is no larger than a good-sized camper van, but in any case I would be living outdoors three-quarters of the time and if my living space had been smaller it would have been no great hardship. On a racing boat you go below for three reasons only: to sit at the chart table, to eat, and to sleep. But since we had the space available we put it to good use by installing a thick bunk—very comfortable, set on gimbals; an enormous navigation table where it would be very pleasant to work, and a galley where you could prepare a meal for five. There was a hanging locker as well, where I would always have my four foul-weather suits and dry clothes to change into. The other advantage of having 86 square feet at my disposal was that I could stock everything below:

food, three-quarters of my tools, my clothing. Everything was within arm's reach and there would be no need to run from one end of the boat to the other to find things. This might seem a detail but it was very important: the entire design of the cabin had been made with an eye to saving time. Food was kept in special lockers under the bunk. I had a bit more than four months' worth of provisions tucked away there. There were very few boxes left lying around—everything had been stowed. The only thing awkward to get at were the rolls of paper towels: I had great quantities of them, but they hardly weighed a thing so it seemed better to stow them forward. Why all these rolls of towels? To protect my neck: every time I went up on deck I would make myself a scarf out of paper towels, a scarf which I would then throw away, which meant I had no wet things on board. They were also useful for mopping up everything which got wet and dirty: dishes, gear, my hands when I'd been working with grease. Cloth handtowels get full of salt and I had no time to let them dry, especially as I had no heating on board. I felt that a heating system would be useless, too great a waste of energy. Also, I wanted to avoid the risk of having a seizure every time I stuck my nose out on deck in the cold of the Southern Ocean—I preferred to get my body used to a fairly low temperature.

Up on deck we designed a watch station for maximum visibility, almost 360 degrees. A wheel, a car seat covered in white leatherette, an instrument panel—anemometer, knotmeter, VHF—all within reach and covered by a clear dome, untinted for better visibility at night. This is where I would spend most of my time, watching the sea and the rigging. The seat could recline, which would allow me to doze, and if for any reason I awoke with a start I could check the instruments immediately. I knew I would be spending nearly eight hours a day there, off and on, with as many hours again right out on deck. So to the right of the seat I had a cassette player installed, and had with me 40 cassettes or more.

Above the seat was a hatch which, when open, made me feel like a soldier peering from the turret of a tank. So I settled in there for a moment after I had stowed everything away. My head and shoulders were outside, my body warm below. There was not a lot of spray and I could see *Poulain's* bow slicing its way into the water. I sniffed the air, the air which was soon to be that of the open sea.

It must have been three o'clock in the afternoon when I went below to prepare a meal. It was my first meal of the day. I had got up at seven, was on board at nine, three hours before departure, but I hadn't eaten because I was too nervous. In any case I have never, even for a local race, been able to get ready to go on a full stomach. It's my way of having stage fright: I can't swallow a thing before departure.

For my first meal on board I threw any old thing together. I was still settling down so I had no precise idea of what to put on the menu and I just grabbed what I could find. Then I went straight back out on deck. It was almost dark; the wind was cooler but still gentle. I was making progress but I knew I would find no strong wind right away. So I put the time to good use making a last check on the instruments. I would have to check them all every day but that first session was rather special. I felt like a teacher taking his class in hand and saying: "And now I trust we're going to spend a good year together."

After weeks and months of going over everything on land I was, at last, actually at the helm; yes, as night fell all stress was gone and I began to feel truly happy.

T HREE DAYS. That's roughly what it takes
a sailor to feel at home on his boat. At
any rate that's what it's always taken
me, and this time was no different. I settled
in slowly: in fact, when still on land I had
seldom been on board. My crew had been
getting the gear ready and I had only gone
down to check things over. I hadn't been
living on board.

My third day fell on New Year's Eve. I
can't stand December 31, can't stand the
year-end festivities and scheduled celebra-
tions; but this time, to be alone at sea was
actually rather amusing and I decided to
celebrate the event properly.

If I were English I'd have put on my

dinner jacket; but I'm not English so I didn't try to dress up—but I did make something of an effort that evening. I got a poor man's decoration together: a paper tablecloth, made from my good old kitchen roll! I put a glass on the table, took a knife and fork and sat down. No question of gorging myself standing up. I opened a bottle of Bordeaux and a small jar of caviar I'd stashed on board, then took the time to toast my bread.

In my mind I reviewed all the New Year's Eves spent at sea, here and there. I remembered one in Noumea with Alain Colas, just the two of us. We didn't have a dime and didn't feel like trying to get ourselves invited by people on land. So we spent the holiday on board, just the two of us, quietly, in a lighthearted, nostalgic mood, chatting about this and that, emptying one bottle after another. Colas told me that night that he was going to buy Tabarly's boat. He wanted to circumnavigate with it—his parents were going to help him, he had a bit of money...And I had listened to him, envious but somewhat afraid he'd do himself some damage—and at the same time I rather wished he would. I had listened and thought, hey, this guy's got some nerve, putting all that money at stake when he hasn't got all that much experience. I knew that I myself would have to wait a long time before I could be my own skipper.

If I thought of Colas that night as I ate my caviar it's because the sea evokes memories of the sea. For me, the world of the ocean excludes all the rest—memories of land stay behind on the dock, just as when I'm on land I have difficulty recalling my time at sea, in a universe so far removed from everything, with other signs, other smells, other rhythms, so intense, so all-absorbing...When I'm sailing, I have no thoughts for my emotional life or my family, but only for my life at sea. Periods and dates may overlap, become confused at times, but ever-present are the successive love affairs I've had with boats.

Still, as I raised my glass of Bordeaux and shouted "Happy New Year" out loud like all the morons revelling from one end of the globe to the other—memories didn't count for much. I was really wishing myself a happy new year to come. I had been underway for three days, well away from the Bay of Biscay, offshore from Lisbon, and the sea was calm. I was rested, relaxed, totally at home, and the weather was much better than if I'd left a month before. In short, I was jubilant on that evening of December 31.

As I stood on deck I could see the stars; the night was clear and I was enjoying a smoke. I thought of everyone out there, stuffing their faces and getting pissed as newts, and I was very pleased to be away from all that. I savored the evening, the wonder of the adventure I was embarked upon, and once again felt happy. I had idiotic thoughts, such as how, each moment, I had never been closer to Cape Horn, since every foot, every inch travelled was taking me closer. Knowing that the entire planet was in the middle of screwing and carrying on like idiots all over the place made me shout with laughter. The next day the pharmacies would be sold out of their supply of Alka Seltzer, but tomorrow I would have better things to do than swallow any of that. I had embarked on something which was a continual high, and if there was anything I wanted to wish others for the New Year it was: "Hey, guys, no nonsense while I'm gone. Don't go declaring a world war or any other such rubbish. Wait until I'm back. I've got a boat I want to take around the world...I'd prefer not to be disturbed during that time."

Those were my thoughts on that soft night of December 31, 1988.

5

B Y JANUARY 2 the New Year's truce was well over: I weathered my first gale off the coast of Madeira. A real little storm it was, with troughs of six to nine feet. The sea is always boiling in that part of the world, with no real shape, short waves, easily murderous. I was pounded with southerly winds of 30 to 35 knots right on the nose. It was the first test for the boat, particularly for my carbon-fiber mast, stepped one week before departure. Until it had been tested at sea there was no way of telling whether it would hold. If it broke, obviously that would mean the ruin of my hopes for a circumnavigation. But the whole boat took it well.

The storm created a great mess, however: a lot of things were badly stowed and came loose to slide all over; I had a rough time of it, standing there in foulies, dripping with drizzle, to put everything back in its place.

But despite that I was proud to see that the boat handled the weather like a trouper. She was a bit too heavy but I knew that with each passing day she would be getting lighter, dropping ten to fifteen pounds a day, sometimes more, between food, tins, oil, diesel...

Already, despite the weight, I could tell she was riding more easily, to a better motion, pitching less. The floats didn't sink into the water as much as they used to when I had the aluminum mast.

I knew that the main structure—the crossbeams, the floats, the central hull, the steering mechanisms, and so on—would all hold up; I had no fears about their reliability because they had all been through real-life tests. So all my fears were concentrated on the rigging. During the 24 hours of storm I spent my time watching the mast, night and day— lighting lamps, walking on deck, checking its profile, its curve...One thing was certain: if the mast were to give, it had better give there and then. Of course the best thing would be if it didn't give at all. It had to finish the course with me. I couldn't afford to let it come to a bad end; I couldn't afford a dismasting, to watch the mast crash down onto the deck and cause all the damage a dismasting always causes. I spent 24 hours with visions of dismastings: if it fell to port, such and such would happen; if it fell to starboard, such and such; if it fell on the float, such and such again...I'd seen enough dismastings in my life to know just what it was like, never quite the same but still similar enough...I went over what to do in case of an accident: do this, that; there's a knife here, a saw blade there, and so on.

I wouldn't go so far as to say that even my dreams were haunted by that damned 82-foot-high carbon-fiber pole, but I was always aware that when you sail around the world, everything depends on everything else. If the mast comes down it's all over, but if your autopilot goes you're a goner too; if the rudder hits some floating debris it's the end— and there is plenty of floating debris off the coast of Africa. Or you might meet an old container still afloat between two waves, or even a whale. The number of potential dangers lurking around a boat like mine is considerable. For the moment the priority was to keep an eye on the mast. It was not a good feeling to have to test it underway, but at the same time there was no other solution. It was part of the job—a job which still leaves much up to contingency, destiny, fate. That may seem a pompous notion, but it reflects what I was experiencing daily on board *Poulain*: there comes a time when things no longer depend on the man, but on his wishes, his desires, his prayers; and circumstances are no longer governed by reason, work, or effort. There always has to be a bit of magic somewhere to keep things going.

The sea is one of the last domains where fate still plays such an important part. When you, as the driver of the locomotive, leave the Montparnasse train station to go to Brest, you know there's little chance of meeting a buffalo on the track. But I could still find plenty of buffaloes on my track!

A mast is not some piece of tree trunk stolen at random from the end of a wharf; it's a highly technical object, well-defined, practically alive in its ability to resist strain.

The pressure can build up to 65 tons at the foot of the mast on a boat like mine. And each new design signals a new discovery, for there is no standard model, particularly with carbon fiber, which has not been used very much until recently. At that point I felt rather confident about the mast: it was built by ACX in Brest and designed together with Bertin Industries. But despite the vast technology, you still end up saying: "By the grace of God," because you can't simulate the strain undergone by an 82-foot mast on the drawing board. Well, actually you could, but it would cost far too much and no sailor has ever had that sort of money ... To be sure of my mast I would have had to break three or four before the departure; again, the air and auto industries can afford to break their prototypes, but we can't.

Xavier Joubert and I first had the idea of using composites for marine construction. We started on the *Jacques Ribourel* and the boat paid heavily for it.[6] But thanks to that experience we found ourselves listed in the SNIAS catalogue.[7] It was the first time composite material had left aviation for the sea, in 1980. Nowadays storage containers for rocket tubes on nuclear submarines are made from composites, and you hear pilots everywhere spouting about composite technology. To hear them you'd think it had suddenly become very important because they're just discovering it—but we were ten years ahead, using the means available in the private sector and an entrepreneur's funds. It was one of my proudest moments. I'm glad I had the chance to work with Joubert on that project, and glad that, together with the engineers from the helicopter division of the SNIAS, we managed to apply their technology elsewhere.

It was that technology I admired when I found myself in the gale off Madeira. I looked at my mast and I could say, "They've done a good job, it's going to work, it's going to be fine."

We made it through our first trial with a clean bill of health: no need to worry.

---

6. *Jacques Ribourel* lost her mainmast in the 1981 Observer/Europe 1 Transatlantic Race. (T.N.)
7. Societé Nationale d'Industries Aéronautiques et Spatiales.

B Y JANUARY 6 I had Dakar on the beam, which meant, first of all, that I'd made good time, and second, that I had not been slowed down along the African coast for lack of wind (I'd had flat calm off the Canaries, but for no more than fifteen hours or so), and finally that the trades would continue to move us along and out of the North Atlantic.

By January 6 I'd already covered nearly 2500 miles, making very regular runs: 395 miles one day, 398 the next—an excellent average, representing a speed of fourteen knots with peaks of 31. At that speed the boat left quite an impressive little wake behind her; but one which faded rapidly because the whole point of trimarans is that they do not dig deep into the waves. A deep wake, one which lasts a long time, means that the boat is not moving properly. At a speed of 31 knots there was nevertheless a fine fantail of spray at *Poulain's* stern, great bursts of foam, eleven or twelve feet high, in her train. It was quite a sight but I had more urgent things on my mind than to sit and watch it. Above a certain speed—about 20 knots—with this type of boat and a beam sea, if you make a mistake at the wheel you're going to compromise your stability, and then you can be sure of a capsize. I needed to focus all my concentration on steering, so instead of looking back at that lovely sight I kept my eyes straight ahead, watching the way the bow met the waves, to get *Poulain* to surf and thus move as fast as possible. I wore goggles to keep the spray from hurting my eyes: salt water at 30 knots makes a painful projectile. And after a while you could get so many salt crystals in your eyes that it would blind you. I tried to protect my face and the rest of my body, because at times the fine beam sea of the trades would send great showers into the cockpit. The water was cold, not lukewarm, and I had no way of getting rid of the salt. I did have a helmet on board, a fine fireman's helmet with a visor, but I was saving it for the coldest weather. So for the time being I preferred to use my foul weather gear with the hood pulled tight and only my goggles sticking out. It was almost too warm but with nothing on underneath I could bear it.

Since my departure I had been able to keep up an impressive rhythm, without having to submit the boat to any unnecessary risk or stress.

I was approaching the equator, which meant that once I crossed it I would have one-ninth of my course behind me, completed in good time and at no cost to myself or the boat. The only thing that bothered me was a slight problem with my electric autopilot; it was beginning to show signs of wear. I would have to use it sparingly, with the consequence that I would have to make more use of my hydraulic autopilot, which would in turn increase my use of electricity. I had planned to run the generator for a total of five hours a day and have it going roughly every six hours to supply the autopilots. I had counted on using very little electricity on this north-south passage, but it wasn't electrical current that worried me, it was the fuel consumption. I had to remind myself constantly that energy consumption on the boat had to comply with certain technical and theoretical realities: the boat had to be regulated over a four-month period, and it was vital that I stay within the norms. This was not something which had been worked out sitting on a barstool between shots of pastis; these were serious projections which had been calculated on the basis of careful reflection, with knowledge of the boat and the gear on board. I did have a safety margin, of course, but I could not afford the luxury, particularly at the beginning of my journey, of going beyond the norms. If I did, the price to pay before arrival would be very high.

And yet I was not worried. The fact that the boat had been going so well since departure gave a strong boost to my morale. When my daily average dropped I allowed my attention to wander from the wheel: I took off my foul-weather jacket and lay stark naked on the deck to get some sun, knowing that once I was past the equator the temperature would begin to drop day by day and I would be in for a long, cold spell.

So there I was, lying naked on the deck, caressed by the sun, happy as a lord, really content. This circumnavigation was not some sort of challenge I'd set myself—in fact I had never set a challenge to anyone. Quite simply, what interested me was the circumnavigation itself. It was the logical continuation of my sailing life, which had started off in multihulls 20 years previously with Colas and Tabarly. If our profession—because it is a profession—is to lead to something of interest it will be to prove the reliability of the multihull. Besides, I was having a damned good time. But a challenge? No way!

7

JANUARY 8 found me off the coast of Guinea, winds still strong but starting to flag. I was approaching the equator. Senegal was behind me, and with it the clouds of dust: *Poulain* was covered with red sand, very fine red sand which had got into everything and made me feel like I'd just finished the Paris-Dakar race under sail. I hate that stretch of the African coast, where the dust is so thick you feel you're surrounded by fog. You can't see the sun rise or set. You can just barely make it out when it's at its zenith during the day, through a screen of muck which must be 100 feet thick or more. Off Dakar the visibility was no greater than two miles— an infinitely depressing sight.

One of the great pleasures of sailing is to contemplate the sea, to admire the sunrise and the sunset, the shadows on clouds, the wrinkles on the water, the blues, the blue-greens, the pastels...the entire rainbow of colors, capable of arousing in any sailor a pleasure both esthetic and sensual.

I also missed the horizon; I love to look off into the distance and I think that is one of the main reasons I chose this profession: I knew that from a sailboat no obstacle could block my view. For some people the ocean is synonymous with monotony and boredom; for me the ocean is—most of the time—magnificent, and I will never tire of contemplating the line where sea and sky meet in such vast tranquillity. And I know I am not alone to thrill to this primeval sight. In the summer a multitude of men and women of all ages come to the coasts of Brittany to gaze in awe at the horizon and the setting sun; people who spend the rest of the year in cramped apartments and air-conditioned offices. They never see the sun rise or set, so they make up for it during their holidays. It's a vital need.

Moments like this, when the world

beyond us is so powerful that it leads us back into the life of the spirit, are very precious in a lifetime. Wisdom dictates that we must not let them slip by. For millions of years the daily performance of sunrise and sunset has taken place and will continue to do so for millions of years if man does not mess around too much with the planet. But how often can any one of us enjoy that performance? What is one lifespan on the scale of the vastness of time? One second— not even: one-tenth of a second! Nothing! And to be deprived of the joy of nature on top of it?

In an urbanized world where man has had the ingenuity to obliterate such magic, other things have been invented to assure survival: gadgets, consumerism. But when I'm out on the ocean, at one with the immensity of space, I no longer feel the need to own anything, or to watch television, listen to the radio, go to the cinema. I surrender totally to the fascination of the universe around me—its smells, its sounds, its existence.

On a murky sea I am overcome, very quickly, by a feeling of claustrophobia. For the entire length of the coast of Senegal I was deprived of one of the greatest joys of sailing.

Now I was travelling along the Gulf of Guinea, without actually going into it as my course was due south. I was far enough away from the coast to have regained my visibility. This was, I knew, a kind of break, a short period of vacation before my arrival in the Southern Ocean. I made good use of it to double-check everything on board, tidy up, do repairs. This general inspection was made even more important by the fact that I had been travelling very quickly over the previous week. The boat had been called on to put in a lot of mechanical effort. I discovered a leak forward—nothing serious, but it was weighing me down with an additional 400 to 500 gallons of water each day. For the time being I didn't mind pumping. To make proper repairs I would virtually have had to stop the boat, and I could not afford such a luxury, time-wise. I was at the edge of a no-man's land, the equatorial zone, and I wanted to get out of there as quickly as possible. Even the slightest puff of wind was not to be ignored.

Sure enough, the next day, January 9, found me in the thick of the Doldrums—as generations of sailors have called this fairly large zone around the equator where the winds drop to nothing: a sort of airlock between the northern trade winds and those of the south; a region of heat, squalls, and heavy black skies streaked with lightning; a stagnant zone, crossed by listless puffs of wind. You can scoot along on port tack at eight knots for ten minutes, then stay in one place for two hours. The sea is often very flat, its surface barely ruffled by ridiculous little splashes in every direction. You feel as if you're in a heat bath, a damp prison, because of the continual showers dropping on you like a curtain. And yet I like this strange world, this parallel universe deserted by birds, in limbo between two hemispheres.

The Doldrums evoke in every sailor's heart the possibility of a dizzying nightmare: what if the wind stopped forever? How would we survive? What sort of world would we be in? The ocean nothing but a vast, smooth surface, a motionless mirror... That is why the Doldrums cannot help but

become infernal after a few days, particularly when you're racing. If you're not out of
there by the third day you can expect your
morale to sink to the depths. Every time a
squall looms, every time a heavy black cloud
comes near the boat, you hope and pray it
will push you along for a few yards...and
then the squall passes you by, sometimes
only 20 yards away, and you're stuck there
like a nerd, pedalling in place. In such a
situation, man can only submit to the will
of the elements.

The positive side was that I knew I was
crossing the equator. The days would be
getting longer since it was now summer in
the southern hemisphere. At the moment I
had exactly 12 hours of night and 12 of day.
But it would begin to shift soon, and in the
far south my nights would be no longer than
five hours. That would help me to sail; I'd
be better able to see what was going on; I'd
have more color, more light. The enchantment of the ocean.

Daytime is the most pleasant time on a
boat. Man is too limited physically to take
advantage of the night. He'd have to have a
cat's eyes. Still, at night sometimes there is

a glow, shades of color, a magic on the sea, when the moon is not hidden by clouds. Then you can see the reflection of the stars on the water, of the moon on the waves. It is infinitely calm and very, very beautiful.

ON THE 14th of January I left Saint Helena on the beam. I'd left the turbulent zones of the equator far behind and the Doldrums were nothing but a memory. The boat was moving peacefully along a sunny ocean, to gentle winds. It was like Brittany in the month of June, only warmer. The weather station in Brest informed me that these light winds—two or three knots—would last a few more days. I made the most of this slack time to put some order in the boat— the wretched leak in the bow to start with. I decided to slow down altogether to ease the pressure so that I could plug the hole more efficiently. As I was going over the entire boat I found I also had water in the starboard float. So I tied myself on with a harness (it was so incredibly stupid: if I slipped I would slide off into the drink) and started pumping out the float. I pumped about 1000 strokes, counting in series. There was a lot of water—it must have starting trickling in before the equator, at the time I was doing my 400 miles a day. But I didn't think it was anything to worry about. I thought I could take care of it; perhaps the through-hulls for the bilge pumps had not been closed properly.

It was as I was pumping that I noticed the autopilot was acting up. It was not holding the course I'd set, and that seemed strange. I began to fiddle with it, and found that the jack was showing worrying signs of fatigue. As I had the time, I had the pleasure of taking it to bits and replacing the jack with a new one.

My head was an inch and a half from the steering mechanism, which was still working; I was flat on my stomach with my shoulders wedged between the deck and the topsides and I had to choose the right moment to move my arm forward and remove the cotter pin from the jack. I felt like I was the prisoner of a nutcracker. In the meantime the boat continued to sail, steered by the hydraulic pilot. I thought I'd change the hydraulic oil while I was at it. Half a turn with the spanner, a quarter turn, a fraction of an inch ... to let the air out. I must have turned too hard because the oil spurted out, and as I couldn't move an inch I got a faceful of it ... The heat was suffocating, sweat was dripping off me. Then the spanner slipped between my fingers and dropped into the deep. When I finally managed to get the drain closed again I was spattered in oil from head to foot. As I wriggled out of the tiny hole I managed to dirty everything I touched. It took me five hours to get it all clean again! In my misery I did have the satisfaction, at the time, of realizing that everything seemed to be working again. I congratulated myself on my mechanical skills, happy too that I'd had fine weather for the duration of my labors. My morale was sky-high. Three hours later it plunged again. The autopilot was back to its old tricks. This time I fiddled with the compass; yes, I was wandering off course.

As long as there were good wind and

regular seas the boat could sail herself, no
doubt because the sails were balanced cor-
rectly; but there in that light wind there
was no doubt that *Poulain* was straying off
course. It should, logically, have been just
the opposite: the boat should have been steadi-
er in calm weather.

And so began an endless relay of radio
communications with the manufacturers and
the suppliers. Didier Ragot finally advised
me to change the brain of the autopilot, but
the idea of manhandling the brain made me
feel like an ape performing an operation
with a rock. I found myself bogged down in
what I hate most: the installation and serv-
ice manual..."Place the brown wire on the
Number 1 terminal spade tag, the blue wire
on the Number 2 terminal spade tag, the
red wire on the Number 3 terminal spade
tag, making certain that the two red wires
are connected by their negative pole to the
upper screw..." There was I in the stern of
the boat, in the bilge, flat on my stomach
and leaning on my elbows, removing with
my screwdriver a thingamajig about which I
hadn't a clue, *not* a clue...

I spent a week down there crawling and

messing around, with no success. I began to think I would have to connect the hydraulic autopilot, something I did not want to do because it would eat up an enormous amount of energy—and fuel.

I had not intended to switch over to the heavy autopilot that early on, but all week long while I was trying to repair the other pilot I had no choice, so the hydraulic autopilot was steering the boat. And then I found another bug. At first it looked as though the hydraulic autopilot was working fine... but in fact it was wobbling. Wobbling because its pedestal was wobbling. Now I really had a serious problem on my hands. My whole circumnavigation was dependent upon the autopilots. At a push I could finish without a mainsail, get back to Brest without a jib, but I could not get back without self-steering. One man alone cannot spend 24 hours a day at the helm in any sea. I know something about it because I once sailed the Route du Rhum without self-steering: for seventeen days I spent 22 hours a day at the wheel. What's more, it was in a temperate zone, even tropical. I could take advantage of the hot weather to sleep on deck, doze next to the wheel. It was nevertheless a terrible ordeal and I had no desire to repeat it in a hurry. Particularly as this time I was headed towards cold weather, a living hell.

I came to the simple conclusion that if I could not repair it by the end of the week, to a point where the boat could be steered in any weather, I would have to stop to get it repaired. And I didn't even want to think about that. *I did not want to envision such a thing.* So I started fiddling with it again like a crazy man: sixteen to eighteen hours a day, trying this part and that, trying to make my own bolts and axles—anything to get the whole thing to stay together. Just imagine: you're no good at mechanical things, no better than me at any rate, and there you are dismantling the engine block of your car, which isn't running and which you have to get going again at any cost. That's what I was doing, sprawled in the bilge, my elbows so scraped that they were raw and bleeding. Yet I felt no pain because the hand I was playing at the moment was so vital for the continuation of my circumnavigation.

Poulain continued on her way as best she could. I managed to stay on course, make some headway; the boat was moving at nearly 90 per cent of her capacities, which reassured me at first, as I thought I wasn't losing too much time. In fact I was losing an awful lot because a day spent messing in the bilges was a day spent neither listening to the weather nor thinking about my route.

That whole week I was like a driver with his hand constantly under the hood. I didn't feel right, even though I had wonderful weather, almost too wonderful, thanks to a vast anticyclone situated above the south of Africa.

The weather did in fact bring things to a head. I was going south at a good clip; down, down, down, and there I was at 47° south. The typical weather of the Roaring Forties was upon me: a strong cross swell from the south, winds of 28 to 30 knots. And there the boat became unmanageable. *Unmanageable.* For 48 hours I tried to stay on course, removing my spinnakers, carrying on with the jib—and still I had to face facts, particularly after a wild and involuntary gybe on a wave: if I carried on without self-steering in the south, with bad weather getting progressively worse, I would get myself killed. I would surely get myself killed.

Four years of dreams, four years of work, four months of preparation—all for nothing because I hadn't been able to make the tests I'd wanted. I had made great daily runs since my departure and now, all of a sudden, my downfall. The way things were at the moment with the boat forced me to admit that my prospects were pretty dismal.

For hours I agonized, because I had set off on a non-stop trip around the world. It was a dream I'd been chasing for years. But without an electric autopilot, or with a hydraulic autopilot that was misbehaving, there was a good chance I would never make it around the world, with or without stops. Or else I could finish feet first. It was mathematical. *I could not carry on like that.*

9

W HEN I DECIDED to turn back I had already lost a lot of time. I had gone south all week as I had obstinately told myself: "It will work out, it has to work out."

I should have decided to double back as soon as the troubles began, but in difficult circumstances a man alone is not always the best judge of how to deal with problems which arise. If I'd had a race manager he'd have been better able to analyze the problem, and would have made me face up to my responsibilities more quickly. My late decision cost me at least 1000 miles. It would take me about five days to get back to Cape Town—five days for nothing, *nothing at all.*

Only lost time; and, as a bonus, an enormous disappointment.

I was sick at heart. I had to stop because of a petty, stupid technical failure for which I had no remedy on board. You simply can't carry the spare part for the spare part, the safety precaution for the safety precaution. The worn-out part would have surfaced earlier if I'd had time to sail the boat before my departure, if I could have just done the scheduled 2200-mile trial run from Brest to the Azores and back.

I was not about to say all was lost, because I hoped I'd be able to repair things properly in Cape Town—but I couldn't help being angry because of preparations being botched for lack of time. I was not able to find out what was wrong with my electric autopilot but at least I was able to locate the problem with the hydraulic autopilot: the pedestal was coming loose...it would have to be rebuilt, and I knew how to go about it. I radioed ashore to let them know of my arrival, and to save time I sent a list of the parts I would need.

When I arrived in Cape Town you could have cut the fog with a knife. I couldn't even make out *Poulain's* bow. I knew there were currents and traffic; I could hear the fog-horns but I couldn't see a thing. From time to time on my radar I could make out a ship, and I could detect the coastline—I must have been less than a mile from shore, but everything was confused. I had only a very general chart for Cape Town. In clear weather it would be more than enough but with this fog it was a torment. If my radar failed to make out an obstacle anything could happen. But I had to keep going, alone, in this unfamiliar territory. With autopilots which were acting up. I had to keep one eye on the radar, one on the chart, one on the compass, one on the fog...you would have to be Argus to see it all at once. I finally drew near land—I could even make out the top of a tower, which meant that the fog was sitting right on the water. Very thick fog, but no higher than 50 feet. I could see the top of the small lighthouse at the entrance to the harbor very clearly. As soon as I was behind the breakwater—I had somehow groped my way in—the fog lifted slightly and someone passed me a tow. I was in a foul mood but I still managed to notice that Didier was there.

And if Didier was there I could be sure the damage would be repaired as quickly as possible. From that point on I could be certain of getting under way again. I would not be stuck in this godforsaken hole—of no interest whatsoever to me.

Didier Ragot had been my first mate for nine years. I met him at the Paris Boat Show. That's actually the last place I would have looked for a partner, but he was introduced to me by a friend who said, "Here's the man who looks after the entire fleet of the Tour de France à la Voile."[8] I said to myself: This must be one super-patient guy, to be looking after 30 boats, 30 amateur sailors who've all got problems, so if he doesn't have a nervous breakdown it means he must be a saint. We were laughing together the moment we were introduced. There's just something about the way the guy looks. You always get the feeling you've seen him somewhere before. After a quarter of an hour I asked him to work with me. We've hardly been apart since.

---

8. Round France Race: a race for one-design, 35-ft. monohulls. (T.N.)

I'm not crazy about human contact. It's not that I dislike others but simply that I care about my independence and peace of mind. Life is not an ongoing election, and as I'm not a politician I have no need to please day and night. Most of the time I'm not the first to speak. It's not scorn, not indifference; I just don't talk to people, that's all. Didier, however, became my chum in a blink of an eye. He's someone I always enjoy being with, whatever the circumstances, wherever we might be. For nine years he's taken care of my boats and dealt with all my suppliers. We've become so close that we don't need to speak—a wink or a nod is enough. In all the years of working together I don't think we've had a single argument. First of all because, contrary to what others might think, I'm not someone who likes to argue with people. I'm not impulsive, nor am I quick-tempered or pigheaded, but I'm not really someone who can be pushed around either. As I'm not the talkative sort, when I do speak, I have a reason for it. When I'm working I like people to trust me enough not to question what I put forward. Didier is the type who does what he says he'll do, and when something goes wrong it's because there really is no way it can work. To err is human, but Didier's margin of error is much smaller than that of anyone I know. He's extremely competent, and that's why I felt certain, as I sailed into Cape Town harbor, that my autopilot would be repaired as quickly as possible.

The hydraulic autopilot at any rate—as for the electric autopilot we would, in fact, make several attempts at repairing it, without success. It was impossible to find out exactly what was wrong. As we didn't have time to carry our investigation any further, I would be heading south with only one autopilot left. I would be taking a major risk, but I really had no other choice. It was double or quits: either I would carry on with no further failures on my remaining autopilot and it would steer the boat home for me, or it would act up again and I would have to give up. I would find out very soon: there could be no question of taking on the Roaring Forties without a trustworthy autopilot.

I arrived at Cape Town on January 30 and the repairs took only a few hours. I could reasonably expect to leave on the 31st.

~~~~~~~~~~~~~~~~~~~~~~~~~~~~~~~~~~

But I preferred to wait an additional 24 hours to give the putty which was holding the autopilot together time to dry. Any regrets I might have had about "losing" another day vanished as the weather turned foul, with winds of 35 knots in the harbor, and no one willing to tow me out to sea.

So I was stuck for a day on board, and only on board—no getting off. The rule of the circumnavigation was clear and simple: I was allowed to make stops, but not to disembark. The others—Didier, Christian, Yves—had to come and see me.

I saw nothing of Cape Town. From my anchorage—a buoy at the entrance to the yacht harbor next to a scuba diving vessel—all I could see was Table Mountain, the flat-topped mountain which overlooks the city. Not a building, not a neon light on the horizon; I was at the far end of the harbor. I might have been anywhere else, or even nowhere.

10

I LEFT CAPE TOWN on February 1. There was not a lot of wind but the sea was vile: a swell remained, very short, rushing in to explode against the docks of the harbor. As I left I met troughs of ten or twelve feet. That was a lot, especially as they were less than 100 feet apart.

Leaving port was particularly tricky because I couldn't find anyone who was used to a boat like mine to give me a tow. There was nothing for it, and the fellow who finally agreed to take me out had a rough time. Even with all the good will in the world, and Didier on board to guide him, he had a rough time, because he'd never towed a trimaran in his life. He used too much acceler-

~~~~~~

ation, thinking that the boat was heavy when in fact it barely sat in the water and all its weight was above the waterline. If the captain who was towing me didn't trust me and didn't obey my slightest gesture and forget about his own impressions, which would, in any case, be wrong, we could have an accident at any moment.

We had to signal to each other continuously, having worked out a code before departure, so he would understand to accelerate or bear to starboard, bear to port, keep straight into the wind, go up a bit to the left, then to the right...

At last we reached the open sea and I cast off. I was under my own steam again, and I heaved a huge sigh of relief.

I was relieved but not consoled. My stop had broken my rhythm and I could not help but think about the 1000 miles or more I had lost. A good week. And, in addition, the weather had deteriorated. The smooth sailing I had had before turning back was now just a memory. I would no longer move as quickly or as smoothly.

For one week I stayed at the edge of the Roaring Forties. I was obeying the instructions of Claude Fons, who advised me not to head too far south because he couldn't really tell what was going on down there. An enormous cyclone was brewing over towards Madagascar; its effects would be felt for several thousand miles. It might prove dangerous, and I think Claude was right to dissuade me from heading south at that time. I had no desire to get trapped in the south. There would be no one in that ocean but me. Nothing and no one. There is only one inhabited zone, the Kerguelen Islands, but it's not a good idea to stop there. I would have no friend who could come to the rescue or pick me up, as has been the case during round-the-world races where another boat goes to the rescue of a sailor in distress. I could call, of course, on the radio, but the nearest human being, once I was in the Southern Ocean, would be nearly 4000 miles away. As mine would be the only boat in the entire area, there would be no one who could turn around to come and get me. I was about to sail across the greatest wilderness on earth—alone.

Claude Fons worked on the assumption that I would make southing quickly—that was where the record could be broken—and easting safely, without taking any risks. I have always gone along with that tactic. Multihulls can be incredibly fast sailing from north to south. But in the Roaring Forties where the seas are very rough I would have to help the boat along, as she'd be submitted to considerable strain.

During the week I spent at the limit of the Forties I was, at least, pleasantly surprised to find myself going much faster than I would have expected upon first leaving Cape Town. One day I even managed 420 miles. It was a longer course but, since I was travelling very fast, I managed to keep up a good average. And I was moving comfortably as well; I was not suffering from the cold, and the gear was not taking a beating. Of one thing I was sure: I was doing well.

The reason for my good speed was a particular meteorological phenomenon: around me was a vast, widespread low-pressure system, a fairly weak one, criss-crossed by high-pressure zones moving at great speed— a situation similar to depressions in the

North Atlantic, but in reverse. In the northern hemisphere low-pressure systems move rapidly in the midst of a high-pressure zone. Here it is the opposite. The highs move in the midst of an immense low-pressure zone. And I was in a good spot behind one of the highs; it was as if I was stuck to the tail-end of the high and I took advantage of its warm northerlies, flying along on a manageable sea.

For a week I was really cozy, safe from harm, and I listened to music, full blast. I never failed to go back to the same cassette: *Brothers in Arms*, by Dire Straits. Every day I'd listen to at least ten minutes' worth: magical pop, purging my mind, revving me up, keeping me alert. I tossed the other cassettes overboard as I went along...Mozart at 2000 fathoms, Mahler at 3000...

The last two days of that week I was sailing the boat to her limits, a bit like a Formula 1 driver who, in order to win, avoids braking until the last possible moment. I knew that the conditions I was enjoying at that moment would not last long; it was a now-or-never moment to push *Poulain* to the utmost, to try my damnedest to get her through.

The next day I would be in the Roaring Forties. That would be a different story.

O N FEBRUARY 14 the weather conditions allowed me to begin my turn southward, into the Roaring Forties. From there on I'd have two months of it, in the cold and wet.

The auguries for my journey south were good: the wind was out of the north, and there seemed to be no more menacing lows in the south. And yet I was about to get the worst beating of my life. I was thrust almost immediately into winds of 45 to 50 knots. That in itself was nothing unusual, but I was caught in seas with troughs of 23 to 30 feet astern and 16 to 23 feet abeam, with very little distance between the waves. The threat lay not so much in the size of the waves but in the lack of space between them. I had barely two boatlengths between each wave, which meant a wave every 30 or 40 seconds. The slamming was unbelievable; my only possible response was to lift the centerboard so that when the waves hit the boat broadside, they met less resistance, and some of the shock was absorbed. But it was excruciating nonetheless, for me and even more so for the boat.

I had never seen such short cross-seas. Nor did I know the reason for such foaming madness: was it a local phenomenon, or a minor depression which had gone unnoticed by weather satellites? Whatever the reason, the seas were very dangerous and the boat was struggling to get through them. But I had no alternative; there was no way out. If I tried to pick up speed to get away from the waves approaching my stern, the waves coming broadside could put me into a tailspin and a certain capsize. At times *Poulain* heeled over as much as 40 degrees; all stability gone, the boat rocked from one float to the other with incredible violence. Several times *Poulain* was completely submerged by the waves coming at us broadside. Everything which was not lashed down went flying onto the cabin sole. And I had to cling on with both hands for 30 hours or more. Not a chance of even frying an egg; nothing would stay on the cooker. Not a chance of any rest on my bunk—I'd have been thrown out. Everything was flying, exploding all around me.

Several times I lost my balance and fell onto the cabin sole. The kitchen shelves spilled their contents; every hatch, every provisions locker flew open. At least a third of my medical supplies were splashing about in a red puddle of strawberry jam. On my knees I tried to tidy up some of the shambles; it kept me busy. Somehow in the turmoil I remembered to set aside the clothes I would need for survival if we capsized, and I tied them up in garbage bags to be sure they stayed dry.

On deck it was horrifying. The sea was dark green, glinting metallic—the color of the end of the world; a shrieking chaos, hurling itself at the boat from every side at once, breaking against the floats to explode in jets of foam reaching up to the first spreaders, 40 feet above the deck! From time to time the sea slipped away from under the boat and she plunged into an abyss. I would bounce 20 inches off the floor. But the worst was the noise caused by the boat's movements, the vibration of the floats, the shrieking of the rigging. Every wave brought with it the impression of a fist in my gut. Frenzied by the slamming I would rush to the watch station ports to check whether the seas hadn't already torn away part of a float. *Poulain* was being massacred before my eyes. I felt that each approaching wave would be my last, that I would be torn away, to disappear from that point on the chart...

It was one of the rare moments in my sailing life when I felt there was *nothing* I could do. It was like being in the ring opposite Cassius Clay and waiting for him to stop punching me in the face. For 30 hours I submitted to those seas with no other prospect than capsize. For the first time I found myself in a situation where I had no power of decision over anything. With each crashing wave my stomach knotted tighter with fear. For good measure I found, moreover, that my port float was shipping water; close to 150 gallons, which amounted to over half a ton at the end of a 26-foot axis, further increasing my chances of capsize. I also worried about the strain on the rigging and began to dread a dismasting. Worst of all was the knowledge that I would not be able to take the necessary steps in case of a dismasting (i.e. cut the shrouds, get the mast away from the vessel to keep it from holing the hull) in such heavy seas. I stayed at the helm to keep myself occupied, or at least give myself that impression, but I could tell it was not serving much purpose. I was no better at steering than the autopilot. I did in fact manage, from time to time, to avoid a trough, but after six or seven hours at the helm I was so stiff that every muscle, every joint was aching.

My fear was so intense—a visceral, animal fear—that I put on my diver's suit over my silk underclothes. I was preparing for survival. I fastened a long knife to my belt and sealed the aft hatch, keeping the life raft and survival kit at hand. I knew that if I capsized I would have only a few minutes to get into the forward cabin where I would— or so I hoped—be partially sheltered from the sea and the cold.

I almost began to wish that I *would* capsize once and for all: that way I would become an active participant, able to decide what my next move would be, instead of continuing to submit passively, fear gnawing my insides. But I also knew that if I were to capsize in that part of the world, my chances of survival would be no greater than five percent, if that, even if I set off the EPIRB. I must have been well over 1000 miles from the Kerguelen Islands, no one from there could come to my rescue. I was no longer in a potential danger zone, I was in the thick of it—pure, absolute danger.

And still I believed that after all my time at sea I knew something about it. I've been through hell and high water—in the path of cyclones, winds of over 120 knots, waves of 60 or 65 feet. I split a boat in half in mid-Atlantic. And on previous races I had spent up to four months in the Southern Ocean. So these were not unfamiliar waters to me; moreover, I'd devoted much thought to them. But in the midst of this maelstrom there was no longer any knowledge, any experience, nor any technical solution. The only response left was to light a candle and say, "Pray God the boat holds up."

Under normal conditions ocean racing is not left up to chance; the risks are calculated. Very often emerging danger can be negotiated: acknowledged, analyzed, then finally overcome. But this time there was no negotiation possible; the danger was massive, overwhelming. Man is powerless when confronted with such danger. He has reached the limit of his courage and his ability. At times like this you feel that the ocean is rebelling and ordering you to leave: "Get out! Don't stay here!"

These hours remain the worst memory of my sailing career, as well as the greatest humiliation of my life, because I was so *powerless* to do anything. I had thought myself to be a strong person, both morally and physically, but faced with the recurring fear of death during those 30 hours I was as naked as a worm. Thirty hours of misery and insanity, and I was reduced to the state of an animal. In warfare, at least, you can answer back...you can get some comfort out of the fact that since you're a goner anyway you may as well shoot down your enemy. The only hope, in my situation, was that it would stop. This was hope founded neither on sailing skills nor on my boat, but on the indifferent hand of chance or fortune.

I was so frightened that I prayed. To make it through this wild and hostile region there was no one left but God. Man can be strong when he has his pride, but not always when faced with something as vile as this. And here I was in the thick of it, by Jesus and Mary and all the saints! Reduced to asking the Good Lord to wipe clean this little corner of ocean so that I could get through, at last.

If I did make it through, this time, it certainly wouldn't be thanks to my experience of the ocean. So there was nothing else left to me: only chance or divine grace.

12

WHO WILL EVER KNOW whether my prayers were heard? The fact of it is that I made it, more humiliated than triumphant. I always knew that I could lose everything... and even so, I was not about to change my way of seeing things because of what had happened. I've always believed that life is only lent to us; if it were given to us, it would be up to us, and not fate, to decide when it is to come to an end. The only way we have of deciding is suicide; we cannot decide in any other way. We are simply tenants, acting on the strength of our knowledge and within the limits of our understanding. But we never know a great deal, and understand even less.

Because I've always been convinced that life is fragile, I've always looked for a lifestyle that would cause my heart to beat faster. So I'm not just some fool who's set off blindly and suddenly found himself confronted with fear. I am a fool all the same, though, a fool who *knew* he'd be scared out of his wits in the Southern Ocean...but it was a bit more than I had bargained for: I had landed myself in a situation where it was impossible to take any action. To be impotent, overwhelmed by events—that was my humiliation.

Several times during my ordeal I tried to relax and rid myself of stress by following the advice given to me by my trainer before departure: to lie on my back and breathe deeply from my stomach. Several times I tried to distract myself by concentrating on my body in order to tame my galloping imagination. I was unable to stem my fear, but at least, through these concentration exercises, I was able to fend off the panic and discouragement which might have caused me to let go of the wheel. But there remains, like a memory made flesh, the bitter taste of my humiliation.

And then, slowly, the elements grew

calmer, the assault less violent. Within a few hours the danger had lessened, finally to disappear. I was then able to think about what I had been through. I was drained. It must have taken me a good fifteen minutes to remove the top of my waterproof suit. What a stink! Like piss... but I hadn't pissed in my pants; it was the acrid smell of fear. In the receding nightmare, I took all my clothes off, despite the cold—only a few degrees above freezing in the cabin—I could not wait for the water to heat. I covered myself with soap, scrubbing with a vengeance. A gallon of fresh water disappeared with my liberating suds. I then tore open a plastic bag containing a T-shirt and long underwear, and I threw away the ones I had been wearing, after using them to mop the cabin sole. Through the port I could see that the seas were much calmer. While heating water for a coffee I went to fetch a bottle of Eau de Cologne from the other end of the boat and splashed myself all over with it. Ten minutes later, a cigarette in my mouth, coffee in hand, I sat at my chart table contemplating the huge mess on board with the indifferent stare of the fellow who's getting ready to go out that very evening.

To celebrate the demise of my fear, I began to eat. I must have eaten for an hour without stopping; chewing slowly and carefully, I took in the equivalent of six or seven meals. I ate to calm my nerves and also because during those 30 hours I had eaten virtually nothing, apart from a few vitamin tablets and half a box of commando rations that I had forced myself to swallow.

Meals, on board, take on an entirely new significance. If the wind shifts, you have to look after the boat before you can begin to think about food. The result is that your meals are irregular and unpredictable. Hunger comes on quickly, according to need and desire, and leaves just as quickly. At sea I eat cheese—on land, never. It must be the need for calcium coming across. Whatever the organism needs becomes a desire, and desire is always good, as it corresponds to a direct need which can be met right away.

Everything you could need is there within reach on the boat but, since you're alone, there's nothing joyful about it. Nor is there a schedule—or even a plate. I wouldn't prepare a thing if my appetite did not arise from desire or need. According to the dieticians who helped me for this trip I had to keep to a certain number of meals a day, simply because the necessity of keeping the boat going is so overwhelming that at times you can forget to eat. You're even tempted to push away your desire. In my case it became a real struggle to force myself. I would concentrate and tell myself, "Okay, it's been ten hours since your last meal; you can't just wait until you pass out." And there you go, one bite for Daddy, one bite for Mummy, don't forget to chew . . .

The real problem at sea is that you don't know when you're going to need that energy. You can't push your organism. It's vital to have strength in reserve. You cannot take the risk of your blood sugar level dropping in the middle of a job.

We set up a regular program with the dieticians. I began to follow it three months before my departure in order to break with my terrestrial habits. For three months I respected orders to eat only at given times, and alone. I was obliged, moreover, to eat noodles at least once a day, at whatever time; they're good for you. Right through to the end of my circumnavigation I stuck to this obligation—with the exception of the infamous 30 hours.

During my preparatory period I also had to try as much as possible to eat the kind of food I would have on board, not to switch overnight from steak and salad to canned food. So I had already included things like almond paste, wheat germ, and bean sprouts in my diet. Even though you don't often get a great thrill out of food on a boat, and everything is good when you're hungry, you do try to make food as palatable as possible. Spaghetti tastes wonderful with just a bit of salt—no butter because there's none on board; no tomato or olive oil either, because there's none or you've used it all up. It's a genuine treat...You end up creating your own little rituals, like eating a cake in the middle of the night between two watches, while you're checking the charts.

I also forced myself to drink: a man loses one and a half quarts of water a day. That corresponds to 20 per cent of your physical reserve. Dehydration can cause a real loss of energy and muscular potential. I always managed to drink between three and seven quarts a day and piss at least half a dozen times to get rid of toxins. At times it was a real effort to drink, but my entire food regime paid off in the end. And it was, in a way, rather satisfying to the senses.

In these extreme conditions, there is an intense rediscovery of the physiological sensation that one is a machine whose physical and mental capacities depend solely on what is absorbed. Throughout my voyage I felt, physically, that I was filling my tank, in the way you fill a gas tank. Or that I was running on empty. And there were times of crisis, such as after my ordeal in the Forties, where I would stuff myself in order to get my strength back quickly. With a tube of concentrated milk, for example—you swallow it in 30 seconds and almost as quickly you feel the effect of the glucose in your blood. Your internal revs get going—and you feel ready to take on the rest of the Roaring Forties.

Poulain during Multihulls Week, 1987

Poulain at the start of Route du Rhum, St. Malo, 1986

Olivier de Kersauson at the helm of *Kriter IV*, 1978

Poulain's crew, Europe Race, 1987

Multihulls Week, Brest, 1987

Poulain, Route du Rhum, 1986

Olivier de Kersauson, Mar del Plata, March 31, 1989

13

THE ROARING FORTIES embody the permanent hostility of the wilderness. It may be summer, but the temperature is that of November or December in Europe. And there is a continuous swell. It's a wild, inhospitable world, but also one of particular beauty and magic. When you sail alone through this part of the world, you begin to feel you are the first man alive, or the only man alive. You are certainly the only representative of the human race for thousands of miles. It's the greatest desert on earth. Even over the Sahara there is always at least one human being somewhere in an airplane in the sky. But here there is nothing. *Nothing.* No men, no planes, no boats, because it's too far south. No one visits because no one lives or works here. No flight corridors, no shipping lanes pass through here.

That is one reason I love this world. It's an interesting place to sail. Harsh, difficult, but fascinating. A sailor will have the same mixed feelings—love, hate—concerning this part of the world, that a mountaineer has for Everest. There is the enchantment of the journey, the wealth of adventure, the delight of solitude. For a sailor, the Roaring Forties are the ultimate experience.

But this ocean kills, something which should never be forgotten. The individual who sets off for the Southern Ocean will find himself in the position of Icarus trying to fly: it has to work—if it doesn't, the fall is fatal. In the North Atlantic, whatever happens, the chances are good that within a fortnight you'll be out of there, even after a serious accident or injury. But there is no way out of here. There is only permanent, relentless hostility. The fact that some sailors come here and find the flight of the albatross graceful and inspiring shows that there really must be nothing else in this godforsaken ocean. I, for one, cannot stand the bird. When friends of mine were lost overboard, those wretched beasts poked their eyes out. This may not be a very poetic vision of nature—but I think the albatross is the vulture of the Southern Ocean, for whom you're just prey to be followed, to be picked at. This is *his* world, a world of ocean and wind, and he deals with everything with astounding ease—never a need to beat his wings as he glides—while to us, below, each wave is a torment: the rigging howls, the boat strains to breaking point and the sailor holds on as best he can. Perhaps my violent dislike of the bloody beast is born of envy. He uses the wind to dominate, and he succeeds. We use the wind—we submit to it, rather—in order to cross, as quickly as possible, a part of the world which wants nothing to do with us in the first place. We're not welcome here; we're intruders. But when things don't go too badly for us, we derive pleasure from the very fact of our presence: we have reached the limits of our profession as sailors.

In any other part of the world when I'm in bad weather I feel, physically, that it is just a bad spell; things will get better a bit further on. Even in the midst of the most violent beatings I took in the North Atlantic I always knew, by looking at the sea, that calmer weather was at hand. In the Forties however you get an impression of universal rage. You cannot expect the weather to ease off, under any circumstances. You have to leave the area for the calm to return. And as it takes nearly two months to cross the Forties, you know that for two months you will be surrounded by this malevolent environment.

On days when everything goes fairly smoothly you have the illusion of living under a benign sky, a delicious illusion of stealing time. The teacher's left the classroom—you can put your fingers up your nose and stare out the window. But when recess is over, you're once again in the daily struggle with the boat against wind and sea.

I often run into fellows who either complain or boast of being caught in summer gales off the coast of Brittany. It makes me laugh because really there's no such thing as a gale in the summer in Brittany. Heavy weather, maybe; winds of 35 or 40 knots; but what to most people is a gale is nothing compared to the average weather conditions day after day when you're in the Southern Ocean. It's another world. Violent colors, greens which are almost black, whitecaps which are not white but grey because there is no sun, no brilliance to make them glitter. It's such an inhospitable world that it's impossible to survive there without a bit of luck. At the same time it's not mere masochism that compels one to go there. When you go in for a sport, you have to take it as far as you can. If you want to be the best in your particular field, it becomes natural to suffer in order to succeed. A marathon runner gives up a lot in order to be a great marathon runner; you can't become one merely by signing up at an Association of Marathon Runners. Someone would find out. A champion runner is a person who has organized his or her life to be a runner. For a professional sailor it's the same thing. When you enjoy this profession, the Southern Ocean has to be part of the attraction. It's human nature to strive continually to go beyond one's known limits. Just the opposite of masochism, I think.

If it were not for this eternal desire to

better ourselves, we would still be in caves rubbing two sticks together to light a fire. It is precisely because one day man chose to confront his environment that human experience has become better, and more interesting. Man is not on earth to live like a recluse but to develop his feelings for and with the world. He does not like to find himself surrounded by things he is unable to do; however, simply because of the way our bodies are formed we are unable to walk on water. If we want to make the most of our world, of the *entire* world in which we live, even if that means simply seeing it, our boats must be built to enable us to sail in waters such as these.

It's love of life which sends us off to wander in regions which are full of risk and yet sublime. And the almost inexpressible beauty of nature. What one feels on the Southern Ocean is very far removed from normal everyday life. Sailing through the Forties is also a way of defying gravity to some degree. There is just you and your boat, alone, in the vast desert of the ocean. There is no greater solitude, but that does not bother me. On the contrary, I think that

reality in life is to be found in solitude.
Everything important you do in life, you do
alone; when you're with others, it's not the
same. Emotion is solitary—you can share
it, several of you can be moved at the same
time, but not always by the same thing or in
the same way. Even in love you travel
alone ...

Words have their own formulas, often to
match our thoughts. When you say circumnavigate, it means, simply, to sail around
the world. As if one could comprehend sailing around the world by saying it! But when
you *have* sailed around the world, you no
longer see it in the same way. Just as I
imagine a man who's been to the moon
and back will no longer look upon us in the
same way. An experience of this kind takes
on an initiatory dimension. As you travel
your soul travels with you; and this travel
shapes your soul. What is literature, anyway? The story of each unique, travelling
soul, as explored and exposed by an author ...
Therein lies its fascination.

14

IT'S NOT SIMPLY a question of heroes who have sailed around the world and then everyone else—even though I firmly believe that sailing around the world allows you to discover another dimension, another type of culture, in the same way that becoming bilingual enables you to discover another mentality.

It bores the balls off me to hear people rattle on about culture with a capital K. You're meant to have read all the authors from Czechoslovakia, and be able to understand Tacitus in the original ... But Culture—doesn't it mean, first and foremost, an exploration of other, different worlds? The loaded question: what *is* culture? It's gaining an insight into other people's thoughts through their self-expression. Insight into their sensitivities, their moods, their humor, their suffering. I think you can find culture in the earth's greatest places of beauty as well. And the Southern Ocean, however hostile it may be, remains beautiful. Travelling through those oceans, those seas, helps to shape an individual. The lessons of the sea are powerful, unforgettable; our earth's hostility is a source of wealth, because it is a source of our own progress.

Man may think he is strong but in fact he is very fragile, very handicapped. If the ambient temperature changes by ten or fifteen degrees he needs to either put on a coat or take it off. The entire world is fragile, for that matter: a plant, too, will prosper or die when placed in a certain spot, give or take a few degrees. Before synthetics were invented man had to steal the skin off a bear, which proves that he has had to rely on intelligence alone for survival in the face of hardship. Otherwise, he would never venture outside, and would remain safely in his den. It's because hundreds of thousands of human beings, over generations, have worked, thought, and taken risks, that our planet now seems less inaccessible. Nowadays you can climb to the top of Mont Blanc and be back down again in the space of five hours. The first expeditions to Mont Blanc in the 18th century lasted for days...

The sea is no different. When I first crossed the Atlantic 30-odd years ago not many of us had succeeded in what was then considered to be a major exploit. Yet nowadays the North Atlantic has become a virtual marine highway for sailors of all stripes. Some day it will be the same in the Southern Ocean, because throughout our history we have sought to reduce earth to a mere nugget, held captive by knowledge.

It seems to be fashionable these days in both commercials and news broadcasts to show images of our planet as seen from a satellite, as if to prove that we've finally done it—Earth has been entirely domesticated by man. Nothing new left to discover -- we've been right round. There's some truth in it, and yet at the same time it's not quite true. Africa, Asia have been explored, gone over with a fine-tooth comb, but the world of the oceans remains full of mysteries. Our knowledge of the oceans is at approximately the same level as our knowledge in the space industry: we do know a lot, but a disaster can still strike at any moment. Obviously a rocket like the Ariane is more sophisticated than a multihull with a carbon-fiber mast, but then the control instruments which the engineers of Kourou[9] have at their disposal are similarly more sophisticated than those available to sailors. So there is a balance: Ariane can goof up from time to time, just as I could capsize in the Roaring Forties. What have I got to guide me? Electronics— satellite navigation instruments, radar—all of which represent enormous progress, there's no denying it. But when the problem of survival is there staring you in the face, instruments no longer have the edge on the sailor's own memory.

When you're used to living outside, the sky, with each passing hour, each new day, is like a familiar face whose every expression you can interpret. You understand the evolution of cloud formations because you've been watching them closely... You've become aware of the blue changing shape above

[9]Launching pad for the Ariane rocket, in French Guyana. (T.N.)

your head; there are nuances which you've come to recognize and analyze. You can then evaluate each nuance as precisely as the policeman standing every day at the same intersection can tell you whether there has been more traffic today than yesterday. When I'm out on the ocean I don't see the blue ocean that most people imagine; I see changing colors. Sometimes I have such a range of colors imprinted on my mind that a certain sea is like the face of someone I have not seen in ten years or more. These imprints are ripples, ruffles, the size of the waves, the small crests which look familiar —part of my culture.

If I could live a thousand years I might get to know all the seas. My trial in the Roaring Forties—the dread, the anxiety, the fear of death—taught me more, made me richer in my knowledge of the sea. I may have been carrying with me the memories of still more dangerous seas, whose shape was familiar to me; but I had never before encountered such a sea as that one. I found myself staring into the face of the unknown. And my trimaran withstood the test like the very devil. They might be able to build boats that are faster than *Poulain*, but it's going to be a few years before they come up with a challenger capable of surpassing her on what she'd experienced. There's not a trimaran anywhere in the world today capable of doing what *Poulain* did.

15

ON FEBRUARY 19 when I emerged from the storm, I had virtually lost all sense of time; not so much because of what I had been through, but because of the fog which had settled around me and which persisted, now that the seas had finally grown quiet. A thick, woolly fog, enveloping me like a tunnel. I could check my wristwatch or the ship's clock at the nav station; I could consult my navigational instruments, which also indicated the number of miles sailed each hour; and I could log each attempt I made to radio for weather forecasts, at whatever time. But I had lost my horizon in this thick fog. I could no longer see the shape of the waves; at night,

there were no stars. The boat moved along—
I could see she was sailing and making
headway but I had no sensation of forward
movement. It was a bit like driving a car
with a windscreen in frosted glass. I could
no longer feel which way I was headed. I
had the physical sensation of being in a
space with no landmarks. What made it still
more unreal was that I was moving east,
and rapidly. I travelled through greatly var-
ying nuances of daylight: every day, between
morning and night there might be changes
in the light every half-hour or so. Usually
when the sun set I would look at my stopwatch, but in that fog it was no use. I must
have had a visibility of less than 100 feet. I
could not see the bow when I was in the
cockpit, nor could I see the masthead when
I looked aloft!

I was like someone trapped at the bot-
tom of a well, cut off from the rest of the
world, for whom time has no markings
beyond those of an internal clock, punctuat-
ed by hunger or sleep. Out of habit I continued to log the hours in the logbook—I never
went for more than an hour and a half
without making an entry in the log—but it

was a totally mechanical gesture. I didn't feel I was really *here*. All my radio communications seemed equally surrealistic. My world had become so obscure and isolated that as soon as I replaced the headset I felt I had just re-lived some memory.

I pushed ahead because I knew I had to. I had to get out of the Roaring Forties as quickly as possible; out of this treacherous, dangerous, evil Indian Ocean. It was on this leg of the 1974 Whitbread Race that Dominique Guillet died. We'd been the best of friends wherever we went—all the seas, all the adventures ... Since Dominique's death I had come to realize that a beautiful, wild ocean is not merely some splendid fairground roller coaster, but something which can kill.

In addition to the fog I had terrible seas. The boat was moving swiftly, but the region was one of breaking, seething waves, endangering *Poulain*, putting her at greater risk of capsize. The fog, with my tendency towards claustrophobia, was a real treat—a prison, a cottonwool well where nothing happened outside my inner circle, the 86 square feet of my living space. Outside, nothing—a soft fluffy element which made me believe—which deluded me into thinking, wrongly—that I was protected. At the same time it was very disturbing: I could not tell whether I was in the air or on the water. I no longer had my feet on the ocean—I had become some sort of satellite—blind, deaf, and bored as hell, because cotton is incredibly monotonous. It was like the red dust along the coast of Africa; I had once again lost that special joy of cruising, being able to observe the sea and the sky, the scowling countenance of a cloud you see at four o'clock and which has changed its shape by five—a change that might give you a clue about the approaching weather or about the winds you will meet.

I knew I was at sea; but all the usual signs were missing, and in such circumstances you begin to think that danger might be lurking nearby. From time to time I switched on the radar, without great conviction. Could it pick up the unexpected obstacle in time? In any case I didn't have enough fuel to leave the radar on all the time, so it wasn't much use just turning it on for short spells of two or three hours. Finally I left it on stand-by and stood with my eyes wide open, desperately trying to see something, anything, in the fog. But my only perception of the outside world was to be found in the few moments spent at the chart table. There at least I could see clearly the shapes of Australia and Tasmania: the only signs still visible of the world out there. It was a strange feeling.

Nothing came on board from outside —there *was* no "outside." When you're at sea, if you don't bring something red on board you won't see the color red for your entire journey... except for the sunset. If you don't take any music you won't hear a single melody. If I hadn't taken a radio I would not have heard a woman's voice... Yet on land in one day you absorb a multitude of colors, shapes, sounds.

My surroundings existed only in my imagination, and I knew I would be better off keeping a check on those imaginary visions: better not to think of icebergs, whales... I mustn't start imagining some nasty trick Nature might or might not play and which I had, in any case, no chance of averting. In that part of the world boats constantly sail past unseen dangers which they manage, unwittingly, to avoid. I recalled hitting a whale in the Indian Ocean with *Kriter*, passing very close to another with *Pen Duick VI* . . . so perhaps at that very moment I would brush by an enormous whale, or a block of ice. Or bump into them. In doubt I chose irrefutable logic: if I could not see the danger, it did not exist. Otherwise I would have had to stop everything; it would have become a living nightmare. And stopping was no solution either. I had to keep going, whatever the cost. Was there any other way? At least there were no ships; I knew that. One less danger. The rest was in God's hands . . .

The first hours were the hardest at this game. I said to myself, "Christ, you're mad to keep on sailing in this shit!" And then after a while you accept it: "Well, after all, if there is imminent danger, you'll still have time to see it. There'll be some miracle and you'll see it!" And you carry on and one fine morning the fog is gone. You see the ocean again and you realize you were right to carry on. Life is often like that, anyway: rather than dwell on shit that might—perhaps, possibly, you never know—happen, you should go ahead and act. And don't back down once you've started.

So there I was flying along at fourteen knots in the fog and trying to remain calm. I had to try and sleep. For three days I tried in vain to keep a watch on the radar screen and all I got in return was eyes like an albino rabbit. I was so exhausted I felt like throwing up. I was seeing double from fatigue. At that point I decided I could no longer sacrifice my sleep. Rather, I would force myself to relax and eat well, with one requirement: remain lucid. At least that way I would be rested should there be an accident!

* * * * *

During my blind man's vigils, during that journey out of time, with no window on the outside world, I let memories resurface— memories of beloved faces, secrets of the soul. I felt so far away, almost dead in my netherworld of fog. Shouldering my bundle of dream and pain, I was like some soul wandering the ocean at the boundary between the living and eternity. I had forgotten the boat, it had become an extension of myself. And yet it was there, alive and real in all of its 75 feet. *Poulain's* history came back to me, and with it one of the greatest joys of my life:

It was two o'clock in the morning at Castel's. In the noise and excitement of the Parisian night I was feeling down, staring at my glass of Perrier. I had no reason to feel that way, however—I was in the company of people I appreciate: Jean Castel, Jacques Martin. We'd been talking sailboats for at least two hours. Hervé Rigaud, a fellow I knew slightly, came and joined us. He was director of communications at Poulain Chocolates. He asked how I was.

"Bloody fed up."

"How's your boat business doing?"

"Not very well, it's taking forever."

"You should see my boss."

"Yeah, really. I called him like you told me to ... three times. He never called back. He's a jerk. Let's change the subject."

The next day at ten in the morning my phone rang. It was Rigaud's boss!

"Hello! So I'm a jerk, am I?"

"No! Well, less of one than I thought, since you're calling me ..."

Philippe Midy—that was his name—
started laughing over the line.

"Listen, you're right, Olivier, I should
have called you but I had a tremendous
amount of work. We should meet. Let's have
lunch together next week, if that's all right
with you."

We fixed a date. To tell the truth I didn't
expect a thing. Four days later I called the
offices of Midial-Poulain to confirm our lunch.
The secretary told me that it would take
place at their offices. Already it seemed as if
it was off to a bad start. Midy must be
feeling sorry he'd invited me. He was going
to squeeze our meal in between two ap-
pointments, at his office. The meeting would
be useless and I'd be wasting my time.

On the appointed day everything seemed
to indicate that I was right. When the CEO
arrived he was carrying a copy of *Mémoires
Salées*, my first book, where I explained, at
the end, my plan to sail around the world.
He said: "Your book's not bad, but I'm not
at all interested in your multihull-round-
the-world business." Midy was surrounded
by a number of colleagues. I looked at them,
one after the other, and instead of persuad-

ing myself that I shouldn't stay here and have lunch with this bunch of buffoons I had to admit that they did look intelligent. There was no way, I thought, that people who were qualified to run an industrial concern of that importance could fail to see the promise of multihulls, especially as they liked boats. So what—I would stay. I had to make them understand. It might be of no use to me, but at least I would get my message across, and in a year or two another sailor might benefit from it.

So I was relaxed by the time we sat down. I had changed my challenge: my only goal at the time was to make these potential backers understand the magic of the multihull. I talked without stopping. They had finished their first course before I had even started on mine. But I could tell they were listening. I told them about my fifteen years of experience—the risk, the inventions, the failures, the shipwrecks, and, above all, the progress made in our sport. We had doubled our speeds in fifteen years. I described the whole sailing scene—the skippers, the sponsors, the races. Philippe and Antoine Midy asked very pertinent questions. I could tell they understood. I no longer felt I was wasting my time. They in turn described how things worked at their firm. I didn't pay too much attention. And then, at one point, Philippe Midy asked me what the procedure was for drawing up contracts with sponsors . . .

I told them a few of the horror stories—how the president of a famous company would commit himself in public then withdraw in private. "We don't do things that way," they countered. I agreed distractedly and carried on with my explanations. We had got to the cheese and I was in the middle of explaining the cost of this type of operation when Philippe Midy interrupted me:

"Okay, Kersauson, you've got your boat!"

Silence. Everything came to a halt.

Through the smoked glass the sun shone on the waters of the Seine. I looked at my companions one by one, trying to fathom each expression. Their eyes said the same thing as their words; they seemed moved—or was it me? Silent, my eyes on the shimmering river, I had the impression that the walls were vanishing and that I was already on the ocean.

I looked round their faces one last time. It was true, it was really true! I'd never known such sudden happiness.

Ten minutes later I was dictating the calendar of operations to the financial officer and the general secretary of the company.

At the end of the afternoon I left the company offices. Alone at the wheel of my car I stopped at an intersection and looked around, amazed, at a world which, for me, had changed color.

16

SLEEP, LIKE EATING, obeys a very particular set of rules on board ship. The rhythm is no longer the same as on land. Sleep becomes voluntary, and is always tributary to a physiological state of fatigue; but it also escapes the routine of life on land, with its very definite times for getting up and going to bed. Sleep on board adapts to the rhythm of the boat, and most of the time it is regulated by the subconscious. It's the type of sleep that can be instantaneous: as soon as you disconnect all your personal alarms, you can fall asleep in a second. You also wake up in a second. It's somewhat like fainting: when you awake you feel you have been frozen in time. You never wake up groggy; you're fit to function right away. It's also very fragmented sleep: on this circumnavigation I spent three months with an average of three hours of sleep every 24 hours. Yet there were times, on the other hand, of crisis—in the fog of the Indian Ocean for example—when I would concentrate on the necessity of sleeping: instead of sleeping an hour and a half after ten hours of activity I was content with no more than an hour and a half of work on the boat in order to spend the rest of the time recuperating.

After ten days or so at sea this particular rhythm settles in by itself. But when you're going away for a trip of four months you're better off getting your body prepared to endure the rhythm beforehand. That is why, just as I had got my body accustomed to a certain diet for solo circumnavigation, I trained myself over the three months before departure to sleep as if I were already on the boat. I worked with a trainer, Denis Cellier, who specialized in the physiological preparation of various athletes, in particular Formula 1 racing car drivers. He supervised the implementation of both my diet and sleep patterns.

Real preparation for a solo circumnavigation also requires you to forget the habits of a typical day: you have to learn to eat when hungry and fall asleep abruptly, in the middle of the day for example. You can do it through yoga, by training yourself to breathe deeply and bring about a complete relaxation of the body; then you wake up to go off and do two hours of bike riding across country. There are a certain number of rules which must be respected: very little wine, no coffee or stimulants, ever; but a minimum of two quarts of water a day. When Denis Cellier was not there he would phone me day and night to make sure I had drunk my two quarts of water, spent two hours riding my bike through the countryside, and done my sleeping exercises.

The discipline I developed in those three months served me well for the entire crossing: I was able, when I most needed it, to relax completely and cut myself off from the problems I encountered in order to concentrate on my physical state as well as my morale, and bounce back, refreshed, to ex-

amine the problems and take the right deci-
sions. For a solo journey lasting four months
the ability to control one's body is extremely important.

Complete control is impossible however.
There are times when sleep becomes an
obsession—when, for example, you're so tired
that you can feel the need for sleep in your
very bones. And yet you know it's not a good
time to leave your post at the helm or the
nav station. You're so afraid you won't wake
up, you'll sleep too long, you say: "I've got
to get farther, I can't go to sleep without
shortening sail, and if I shorten sail I won't
move, I'll never get the hell out of these
Roaring Forties..." You have to be very careful not to get caught up in this vicious
circle. There's a stage of fatigue you must
never pass. Beyond it you might not be able
to function properly, you might even become
dangerously clumsy, when the slightest movement becomes complicated. After 30 or 40
or 60 hours without sleep you can run into
another phenomenon familiar to many long-
distance singlehanders: hallucination. You've
got to do everything you can to prevent
crossing that threshold.

That was one of my great fears during the circumnavigation. So the few times I let things slip too far (when I hadn't slept for 50 hours or so) I would recuperate in the same way a diver decompresses: in stages. I would start by sleeping in such uncomfortable conditions that I would be sure not to oversleep. I would, for example, lie down on the cabin sole to do some decompression exercises; then I would go and sit in my seat at the helm and doze for an hour or two. I would call it my filtering stage, the way you filter impurities. Only then could I go to my berth in search of genuinely refreshing sleep. But even then I took care to limit the amount I slept. When you drive, you can pull over to the side of the road and take eight hours of sleep. At sea there is no side of the road and no sailor has the means to steal a long, deep sleep, in hopes of forgetting everything. I would switch on the alarm horn—a sort of World War II submarine horn—and program it to wake me up after an hour or an hour and a half. The horn could not be turned off unless I left my bunk at the opposite end of the boat. Its siren was so traumatizing that after a few days I could tell when it was about to sound and I would wake up just a few moments beforehand in order to switch it off! As soon as I'd switched it off I had an overwhelming mad desire to return to my bunk. Three minutes later the feeling would fade; I would heat up my decaf, check the generator, the chart, the dead reckoning, the winds, and off I'd go...

All the time I was in the fog—ten days or more—I would divide my time between periods of sleep and moments devoted to myself, drifting back towards the shores of childhood.

As there was nothing else beyond me and my memories I found, to my surprise, that I was talking to myself. At one point I called myself, "My old buddy!" It was the strangest impression... When I was small—four or five—my father would call me that, and there was I, 45 years of age, speaking to myself as my father had done, to encourage me. I was born in 1944, a war baby. I'd had rickets in my childhood—wasn't strong at all, was sick all the time, had trouble running on my bandy legs—so my father, to cheer me, would say "Go on, old buddy!"

I had to laugh, thinking I'd lapsed into second childhood, and yet it was touching. Remembrance opened to other memories, images resurfacing, bringing back periods of my life in a different light, as I'd never seen them before. Memories, emotions, swept over me at that moment as if I were experiencing them for the first time, perhaps because never in my life had I been in such extreme conditions. Normally, other people step into our lives and interrupt our history, because we are obliged to integrate them into our world; the threads of our intimate history are stretched, chafed, worn thin. Yet here it was as if my story had been rethreaded, as if no one had ever interrupted it. Being there, cut off from human contact, made me feel like a child again. It was not some mental vacuousness or moral or intellectual wandering brought on by I don't know what, the perverse effects of solitude... On the contrary, I found myself on my own true journey, the journey of childhood, the journey towards self. And there was always the same problem bubbling to the surface: was I fulfilling what I had promised myself, more or less consciously, as a child? I answered "Yes," since I was doing what I had always dreamt of doing. And so I was unworried and happy as I emerged from the fog: I might have wrinkles, but I felt I had found, once again, that same innocence and purity of childhood.

17

ON FEBRUARY 24 I cleared the second of the three capes, Cape Leeuwin. I was exactly half-way around the world. I was not yet out of the Indian Ocean but I'd covered most of it. There remained the coast of Australia, then Tasmania. Things would improve from there on. They already had improved, in fact, because I could see again. I felt I was gradually returning to the world of mankind—re-entering the atmosphere. Australia was only 1800 miles away. Whatever happened I could always make my way to the Australian coast, quite easily, even if I were dismasted. Besides, I would have every chance of meeting a cargo ship on my way. I was leaving the wilderness behind, and man was closer. The sea was now contained by boundaries, landmarks. I was finally making headway: each degree meant something. And I was pleased to be leaving the Indian Ocean. The sooner I was out of that rotten place the better.

I knew I was not far from the spot where Dominique Guillet had disappeared. We had been there fifteen years ago... That morning the weather was foul—enormous seas had been pounding us all night. I was in my bunk, dozing fitfully, and a few feet away from me the radio was crackling. That was how I heard, from another boat, that Dominique was overboard. The first death of the race. He had been a really good friend, and his crew had lost him. Caught between anger and despair, how can one judge—would we have done better, or done more, in their place? You have to be very ignorant of the ways of the sea to presume to judge in cases like this: We'd been knocked down once or twice during the night, in those tremendous seas, mast in the water. The crew was probably beyond reproach—you couldn't blame them because a man fell in the water. No way. If they were not able to rescue him, no doubt I would not have been able to rescue him either.

It depressed me to think back on it, but on the other hand I had to admit, once again, that I had been lucky: here I was, fifteen years later, sailing past that very spot on my trimaran. Life had been good to me— but how much did that depend on me alone, and how much just on fate? In everything we do—in every successful venture—struggle certainly counts for something, but if luck is not on our side, nothing happens.

In the solitude of the Southern Ocean such thoughts take on greater intensity, greater presence. There is no one to switch your thoughts onto another track. Forced to turn in upon yourself you say: "In a few years it will be my turn to dig my grave," and you're not sad in the least. It's not a morbid or lugubrious thought. Death belongs to life; one must never forget that, even if there is nothing worse than death. Death is someone switching off the television, stopping the film just when you wanted to find out what was going to happen. Dominique wanted to find out what was going to happen. So did Gillard, de Roux, Caradec, Moussy... We carry on until the film stops. That's all. It is because sailors have taken risks and because the sport has given them their share of shit that we have to continue to sail and take risks. If we don't we're no better than pigs in a barnyard. It's a question of dignity. The dignity of the sport requires us to go the whole nine yards. When we do follow through, as sailors, and thus really live up to our convictions, this might be the only time when, as human beings, we are not too pathetic.

I don't like risk for its own sake. Even stuntmen—the good ones, the professionals—don't particularly like risk. They take incredible precautions. But life itself is a risk. Once we accept that fact, there is no longer any reason to be afraid. In any case, no one has the choice between mortality and immortality. It won't do to say "Listen, it's me, Kersauson, and I'm really sorry, but I'd like you to assign me to the category of the immortals." Once we accept that it simply won't wash, there's no point in behaving as if we were immortal. As mortal human beings, we must choose our risks rather than submit to them.

And I have chosen the risk of the ocean.

ON FEBRUARY 28 I finally left the Indian Ocean behind and entered the Pacific. The boat was sailing well to steady winds, and for ten hours or so I had been sitting at the chart table, waiting for the moment when I would cross the line. I was waiting *just for that*, and so I wrote down in the logbook the precise time when, symbolically, we crossed from one ocean into the other: 11:18 P.M. It was like a door closing behind me and I heaved a great sigh of relief: "So long, goddamn Indian Ocean. So long superstitious beliefs: 'There's always a third time!'" For a long time I had thought I'd be the third on the list, after Dominique Guillet and Jacques de Roux.

"So long, rotten ocean, frostbite, damned Kerguelen Islands, shit-faced albatrosses, ruddy whales, bloody idiots of all sorts, damned hell-hole!" Oh how glad I was! It was only an imaginary line, but as the imaginary is always extremely important in life, the moment we crossed the line I drank a toast, pissed off the stern, and gave that ocean the old finger. It was the sweetness of seeing the gates of hell close before me; it was seventh heaven.

From there on I'd be able to think of my return passage. I had covered half of the course; until then every mile had been taking me farther from Brest. Now every mile would be taking me nearer.

As I crossed the line I changed charts. And what did I see, at the top of the new chart, to the right, nicely spread out? Polynesia! Samoa, Fiji, Tahiti, the Gambiers Islands. I went cross-eyed from staring at that upper-right-hand corner. I had lived for three years in Polynesia, three years of perfect happiness. I was crazy about the place—still am, in fact. In my humble opinion there are only two possible places of interest to a gentleman: Brittany and Polynesia. Those three wonderful years spent in Polynesia filled my thoughts—life in the lagoons; cruising, bare-chested, on a Pacific ocean drenched in sunshine, friends, boats... Names, faces came back, and the entire travel brochure with them.

It had been a tremendous shock to me, arriving there; it was the first time in my life that I regretted not being born in the country I was just discovering. I liked the Polynesians as soon as I met them: there is something about them which strikes a chord deep within me. Surrounded by the Pacific, they are truly people of the sea.

I became so obsessed that I tried to pick up Mahina Radio, hoping to hear the call of the islands, the Polynesian boats speaking to each other. I couldn't get their frequency— so I imagined it, and very soon it would not leave me alone, particularly as my daily life on board was no piece of cake. I had just left New Zealand on my port quarter but I would have to keep heading south until I had rounded Cape Horn. *Poulain* was taking on water and I had to pump. I was pumping like some fool of a bartender on a hot day, while in Polynesia ...

Memories caused my heart to beat with such violence that at one point I was sorely tempted to give it all up, flee the horrors of Cape Horn and head straight for the sun. Ah, the sun, so warm and soothing. I hadn't seen it for a month.

Yet here, south of New Zealand, the sun was making a timid attempt to break through, and the temperature was so mild—it must have been nearly 70 degrees in the sun— that I sat down on deck with a picnic, paper tablecloth and all. That's when I said to myself that I must be a masochist to want to go back into that fog after I'd only just left it. What was wrong with me, wanting to be the Tarzan of the Southern Ocean? There was something perverse about wanting to knock on the gates of hell again when paradise was only 3000 miles to the north! Why not go and find my friends in the lagoons? Get drunk again together, feel 20 years old all over again ... The trap of memory was closing around me. I could see the beaches, almost feel the fine white sand trickling between my fingers, the sirens' call!

I'm not someone who runs on pleasure—at least I don't necessarily go looking for pleasure above all else in everything I do. But in this case I felt I had 3000 good reasons to give up, the two biggest of which were that my boat was taking on water and my electronics were not working properly. If I got another pounding I was not sure *Poulain* would take it very well. The deterioration of my gear could trigger a major breakdown. I could die in ten days' time, and yet here I had the possibility of going to warm my soul in the sun!

For an entire week I lived with this insidious temptation making my life a misery. I took advantage of the fine weather to repair what I could on the boat (my lightning rod had gone; I had a leak in the water pump, etc.) but always there was a voice inside crying out: "It would be so much better to do these repairs in the sun!"

To try to rid myself of this cruel dilemma I made a list of the pros and cons, then read it out loud. I've always done things this way. It's a good method for warding off temptation. It was a good job I hadn't any Tahitian music among my cassettes or I would have cracked, irrevocably, and all my fine efforts to be reasonable would have amounted to nothing...

I tried self-persuasion: "I've got to continue what I've started. I'll be forfeiting everything I've accomplished if I throw myself blindly at pleasure." As a consolation I promised myself that I'd head straight for Polynesia once I finished the circumnavigation. It was a first step in my decision to carry on. Besides, intellectually, I realized there was something not quite right about the idea of going to sprawl in the sand before I had finished the job—a job on which I'd had a lot of people working. That was the second step. Finally, I figured I didn't have a lot of miles left to cover, really. I needed 25 days, if that, to reach Cape Horn; then heading up for Brest would be a simple formality. It was no longer the end of the world. And that was the third step.

So, with each passing day the temptation dwindled until finally it was gone. Time had worked its trick: I understood that I would never again find what I had known in Polynesia; my dreams were born of memories of youth, gone forever. I might, it's true, find Polynesia, and its charm; but I would never find my youth.

What a load of rubbish, I thought. After all.

O N MARCH 7, as I was struggling against
the temptation of heading straight
for Polynesia, I crossed the meridian
of 180° and with it the International Date
Line into the other half of the world, the
half where France is found.

The boat was flying along. I was on the
verge of setting a new record for crossing
the Pacific between Cape Leeuwin and Cape
Horn. A record within a record, in a way.
And, what made me happier than anything,
my passage was made in relatively safe conditions. The boat rose on successive swells
which caused her, every three minutes or so,
to surf along the crests of the waves. In 45
seconds my speed would shoot from 14 to 20

knots as *Poulain* caught the wave, went faster and faster, and then took off. In these conditions the boat was under no physical strain. I was still in the Forties, but it was a beautiful sea, rewarding, with pleasant conditions. It was almost magical, with the giddiness of speed and the amazing elegance of a 75-foot boat skipping from wave to wave. It was a continual flow of delight. At times like that I felt I had an almost sensual relationship with the boat.

You do, in any case, have a physical relationship with a boat. When you set off for such a long time you grow as accustomed to the boat as to your shoes: you put them on in the morning and by midday you don't even think about them—except if they don't suit your feet, or you stub your foot on the curb, or walk into a pile of dog shit. Otherwise they don't exist. A boat's the same—an extension, a tool in your hand.

Very soon—after three weeks at the most on a major passage like this—you're at one with your boat. It transmits all sorts of information, like some tactile limb which your brain accepts without question; data is entered and filed at great speed. There are no surprises; there would have to be an incredibly unusual movement for you to realize that something had changed. Only when the boat changes its rhythm, when you go from a run to a beat, for example, do you change your programming, recalling other things in order to find your balance again. Fortunately this never takes long, and it's almost unconscious.

While you're asleep you are also, unconsciously, analyzing all the boat's movements. Only an abnormal motion will set off the alarm. It's like having someone sleeping next to you while you're driving. They'll only wake up if you slam on the brakes suddenly or accelerate too abruptly. The same is true at sea. Very quickly you turn into a man-boat, a sort of mutant, with the boat as an extension of yourself. This is not the same thing as getting used to the boat, because simple acclimatization is passive, and steering a course is active. It's more a question of knowledge: you end up having completely assimilated the concept of steering. After a while you might be capable of knowing the figures on your dials without looking, simply from the feel of the boat. You become a better sailor, while the boat deteriorates irreversibly. By the end of my circumnavigation the mast, the sails and most of the gear were good for the rubbish heap. But because a sailor gradually becomes more at ease and more familiar with his boat, he manages to make up for this deterioration. Otherwise a solo journey would be no more than a slow, inevitable degradation, ultimately pointless. Worse than that, it could lead to the death of the man and his boat.

By dint of careful step-by-step analysis of each maneuver, before I was actually called on to perform it, I had managed to create a series of automatic reflexes. There was not a single maneuver—except for emergencies on deck—which I had not already dissected before doing it. It's like someone who's about to get up in the morning saying: "First I put my right foot down, then the left, then I put on my right sock, then the left, then my trousers, shoes, shirt, then off to the bathroom ..." It's all done to ensure that nothing is left to chance, and that the movements will be perfectly concentrated. Like commando training, recapitulating: "Right, the door will open at 10:05, you will remove the pin from the grenade at exactly 10:05 and one second," and so on. In your head you write out the script of an action which must be totally controlled. The whole point of rationalizing in a domain where the irrational reigns supreme is to be able to confront the unexpected with your reflexes fully trained. If something unexpected happens, you'll be better prepared to cope with it accordingly. If, for example, the mast were to fall, I would have a number of rules at the ready, such as never going up on deck without my knife at my waist. If I had forgotten it, I would go back down to get it. The same procedure for all kinds of operations—they amounted to real check-lists which I forced myself to respect. At a push I could have made them into a computer program.

All my conditioned reflexes and the confidence I'd acquired in my reactions on board enabled me to appreciate what it really meant to reach the end of the Roaring Forties. The trimaran was moving wonderfully, surfing along the waves. I felt almost sure of my success. I was out of the worst of it, *Poulain* was somewhat the worse for wear, but I had a lot more confidence in the Pacific than in the Indian Ocean, and Claude Fons had nothing but good news for me regarding the weather. So I sailed quietly along, to my greatest pleasure, and strolled up and down the deck, smoking.

I never had the slightest intention of giving up smoking before setting off on this circumnavigation. I never have decided to stop smoking. When I'm sailing I don't drink and I don't screw—so at least I can have my cigarettes. Besides, in the world of boats you're in the fresh air 95 per cent of the time; there's surely less danger in smoking at sea than in smoking in Paris. A little smoke warms you up, keeps you company. So I smoked without overdoing it, very mild cigarettes anyway. I had also taken along rolling tobacco in case I used up my stock. Fortunately I never ran short. There's nothing better than tobacco for your mental health!

20

O N MARCH 17 the weather allowed me to begin my descent towards Cape Horn. I left the Forties to go beyond latitude 50° south. Cape Horn is at latitude 57°. Given the enormous seas of the southern Pacific it's a good idea to leave sufficient sea-room so you can maneuver between the direction of the wind and that of the waves. As you approach Cape Horn the sea floor climbs dramatically from 6500 feet to 400-500 feet. It's shoal-ground where the swell comes crashing in, watched over by steep mountains, 13,000 feet in height, which drop directly into the sea. The mountains deflect the westerly winds and, above all, create an additional current in the water. In heavy weather the waves in this part of the world can run 15 or 20 knots. A boat has to move at least that fast to avoid being slammed, or stalled, or pushed towards the shore. So you have to stay on the lip of the funnel by heading for 58° south at a steady clip. That was why I started to make southing so early, even though I would only draw level with the Cape a week later. It was the right time of year, and there was no point in getting there too early either, as I would only be in time to catch the bad weather and all its attendant dangers.

This was the start of a very gratifying bout of sailing. Terribly physical, but gratifying. My descent was regular, rapid. The seas were rough, the waves very well-shaped, 30 to 40 feet in height, and winds gusting up to 50 knots. It was fine southern sea, wild, blue like steel, blue-black. There was no horizon beyond the wall of waves at my bow. But I had known worse.

This was sailing at its most taxing; for 50 hours or more there were squalls every 20 minutes. They reminded me of tropical squalls, which often roll by in the same rhythm, the only difference being that these were not tropical rains, but hail and snow. With ice for dessert. Very quickly snow drifts formed on deck, making it very slippery. For 50 hours I made my way through squalls which came with an almost metronomic regularity. But I felt fine, in full control of the seas. I put a reef in, shook it out, put it in again, shook it out. After some time, three or four hours, when I realized that neither the clouds nor the air pressure were about to change, it became a huge joke. I knew I had 20 minutes until the next one would hit. Impressive squalls, the snow falling in a straight curtain, darkening the sky. Then blue sky again, then here we go, the sudden darkening—the southern seas at their best, wild and mean as they can be, and which you grow to appreciate once you've learned how to handle them.

It was impossible for me to get any decent sleep. If I took my prescribed hour and a half I would sleep through three squalls, three golden opportunities for the boat to capsize, so I would doze for five or six minutes in my seat at the wheel, and before each squall kept myself as busy as I could. I ate, washed, shaved. This was the first time since departure that I actually shaved every day: it was getting really cold, and when I went below my beard dripped cold salt water all over me. And, I might as well confess, my beard was going white! Not with snow either— it had turned a salt-and-pepper shade which undermined my morale. From then on I decided to shave every day, to rid myself of the self-portrait I had seen in my mirror. I had been looking at myself without really seeing my reflection, and then all of a sudden there I was: 50 days in the Southern Ocean, and with this white beard I looked 20 years older. I'm not one who pursues the cult of beauty, but the whiteness of my beard was a shock because it was such a tangible translation of the passing of time. I was staring at another stopwatch, not the one on my chart table, but one showing the years which had flown by.

There was one other time during my trip when I saw myself in this way, and that was during the infamous 30 hours where I had been so humiliated by helplessness and fear. I had started to jot down my thoughts, but then I felt that merely writing what I felt was not enough. So I filmed myself, a close-up. The image of oneself sweating with fear is disgusting, even more so than any image reflecting the ravages of time. In the horrible mirror, with no distortions, of my face filmed by the video camera I saw myself pushed up against my own outer limits.

"Know yourself," said the ancient wise man. I believe that once you know yourself, and you try not to be too soft on yourself, you are better equipped to come to terms with those around you.

And who are they, these other people? Only reflections of ourselves, dressed differently, with a different skin. Shapes, colors, races, choices, concepts may vary from one society to another, but the history of humanity rests on one vast common destiny. Since the dawn of mankind humans have loved each other in the same manner and have always sought more or less the same things. And despite this our ignorance of our fellow man is colossal, because of the paucity of our intellectual capacities, and because of the wealth and complexity of human nature. And also because the society we live in forces us to put survival before contemplation of human nature. Society is nothing other than a sum total of individuals, and each of us has a story with the same beginning and the same ending as everyone else's. We neither ask to be born nor, as a rule, to die. What lies in between? We have our dreams, suffering, sorrows and, occasionally, moments of happiness. For each person it is a special adventure, unique. Yet we know so little about others, even about those we care for. If we can't be even a little bit honest with ourselves, we'll never be able to truly communicate with others, no matter how long we've lived with someone, at their side. To care for someone and be close to that person in spirit does not require you to spend a lot of time with them. It's useless, for example, to want to "make the most of" someone's presence, as if you could stockpile it for the future. I might have said to myself, before leaving, "Right, I'm going to spend a week alone with my son, to make the most of him, because I may not return..." It doesn't work that way. You can't put time in a jar like pickles. That would be too easy.

21

ON MARCH 21, the first day of autumn in the Southern Hemisphere, I was only 600 miles from Cape Horn. It was now very cold. I had no idea of the exact temperature but the snow falling on the boat did not melt. I wore long underwear and silk T-shirts under my polar suit. I had another suit, made by Cotten in Concarneau, with waterproof cloth on the outside and real fur on the inside. At night I could not go to my berth because of the recurring squalls, nor could I get undressed because I had to go back up on deck to shorten sail before each squall. So, to try to get some rest in a sheltered spot I lay right on the cabin sole, fully dressed, under an aluminum survival blanket. That way I could sleep for five or six minutes between squalls; sometimes ten, never more. From time to time, to give myself an illusion of heat, I would light the stove for a few minutes. And when I was cooking I would leave the burner on a little longer than necessary.

I spent seven or eight hours a day on deck just wending my way through the squalls. The seas were getting wilder, very rough, but there were no cross-seas. I thought I could handle it easily enough. I was making daily runs of 380 miles and thought I could see light at the end of the tunnel: with each passing day the risk of the unthinkable was decreasing. With each passing day I could say, "If that goes, I'll make it all the same, or if that goes, I can still make it..."

Another source of comfort was knowing exactly where I was. Earlier on, particularly when I was sailing through the fog, I had found it extremely difficult to determine my position. Satellites give poor coverage of the Roaring Forties. It is such a deserted part of the world that there is no real need for extensive coverage. I had also brought on board a land-based positioning system called

Omega which can, depending on the station, determine a position in relation to a signal from a transmitter. The system closed down completely during my passage through the Forties: not a bleep, the stations were much too far away. Now, however, it was working brilliantly...

My position was a good one, and I felt reassured. When you approach Cape Horn there is always the risk, at night, that you'll sail too close to the rocks, since there are virtually no dwellings or lights to be seen. There is a small lighthouse, flanked by a tiny wooden chapel, on the summit of the dark headland which drops straight into the sea, but it's not a powerful light. By the time you see it it could be too late to maneuver.

On March 24 I rounded the Cape in exceptional conditions: the sun was shining and the sea was as smooth as oilskin. It was like the Bay of Quiberon in the middle of June. It was cool, the wind blowing a meager two knots, if that! I sailed as closely as I dared to the rocks, for I hadn't seen land for two months. Not a human being in sight, just the island of Diego Ramirez, where a small house nestled against the wind.

A whisper of nostalgia in the air—I was leaving the South. The blue of the sky was very pure, fresh, not a cloud; the world of wind had stopped, closed behind me. This was my third passage round Cape Horn, and I had never seen it like this. How many sailors have seen it in calm weather? Thirty point fifty nine inches on the barometer—that cannot happen too often around here. I had the curious sensation of visiting a peaceful battlefield. The rocks, the giant algae which rose from the depths, all the wilderness of this landscape could not find their usual sustenance in such calm. The boat moved at three knots in waters that were too blue, among the albatrosses floating on this enchanted lake. There was no swell; only the sun glistening on the water. This silence of the sea was like the silence of cemeteries. I watched the jagged coast closely, as you watch the faces of those you are not sure to see again. Other faces, those of the friends who disappeared at sea, filled my memory. I thought of those I had known personally, then of the others. All those who would have been saved had the weather been this kind as they made their attempt at this murderous cape. Broken boats, masts ripped away, the cries of those who clung to their spars... and the furious sea, destroying everything. This place conjured up implacable visions of death and human suffering. I was alive, so alive, after two months in the Southern Ocean; yes, I reminded myself, I had indeed been lucky. But my intuition told me that the winds had abandoned me, auguring poorly for my northbound passage...

I was moving so slowly that I decided it was a good time to change my mainsail. I had thought I would change it only once I reached the Atlantic. I had two mainsails with me: one without battens for the Southern Ocean, which would allow me to handle it more quickly, even to cut it loose if necessary; the other with battens, for the homeward passage. On a boat this size it's a tremendous job to fold one mainsail and set another. It took me all day, but it was such a fine day that I never noticed the time go by. The visibility was phenomenal. I could even see the mountain peaks at the tip of South America. Everything seemed to have stopped.

~~~~~~~~~~~~~~~~~~~~~~~~~~~~~~~~~~

I felt I was on some winter sport holiday with those snow-capped peaks for a horizon. After what I had been through in the south it would be dishonest to say I was sorry I didn't have a devil in my train. I savored this almost incredible good fortune. There might be fine weather at Cape Horn three or four days a year, no more. A true miracle would have been a passage with a touch more wind, ten knots for example, to increase my speed.

At noon I paused in my sail-changing to take a little break on deck in the sun. The Cape was already far behind us. The first time I'd been around was nearly seventeen years before as Tabarly's first mate. The second time I was the skipper on *Kriter*. And today I was alone on a multihull. Would I be back a fourth time? I wasn't sure—I had the impression that I had come full circle.

But I wasn't home yet. I had left the danger zone of the Forties, but I could still come to grief in the last quarter of the trip, the thousands of miles between me and Brest...

Particularly as my electronics were acting up. If I had to head north through stinking calm weather I had to have my electronics. If my wind indicator packed in, for example, I'd be in trouble, especially when I'd have to keep a constant watch for wind if I hoped to move forward. I could not allow the remainder of my trip to be ruined for a bloody stupid thing like this. Even if I lost a few days to get it fixed it would cost less than having to drag along in light winds, stuck at the wheel 24 hours a day. The electronics could help me to gain time, even if I had to stop for a day. What I lost in time I would be able to recover through careful navigation and in avoiding fatigue.

So I decided to stop a second time, in Mar del Plata, Argentina.

22

I REACHED MAR DEL PLATA on March 30, around midnight. It took me much longer to reach port than I had expected. Not long after Cape Horn the wind kicked up, but not from the right direction—I had it on the nose and it was a struggle to make northing. Then I ran into a series of very violent squalls, infernal storms with streaks of lightning across the entire sky, hardly reassuring. I had brought a lightning rod system on board, but I had lost it. I had the feeling that if lightning struck I'd first of all get my balls fried, then soaked. My carbon mast was terribly conductive...

As the majority of my antennae were live I switched everything off during the storms. And squeezed my feet together. The most murderous thing in a storm is to stand with your feet spread, because in fact lightning rises from the ground. That's why you often see cows felled by lightning in fields, because of the large space between their legs, which causes a fatal difference of potential. So I lived with my legs together and it was no fun at all. Particularly as for four or five days I was battling nasty seas, with winds from every direction constantly obliging me to adjust my sails or course. It was like a trapeze act.

In addition to the lightning I dreaded the appearance of the *pampero,* a local specialty on that coast—a sort of extremely violent mini-depression capable of stirring up vile seas. Philippe Monnet had run into one which had forced him to flee at breakneck speed to the south, through extremely dangerous cross-seas; he had been close to capsize. He was so certain of it at one point that he jumped overboard to be on the right side when the boat flipped over.

Whatever happened I knew I would get out alive. That was the main difference between the Southern Ocean and here. Since rounding Cape Horn I had the feeling I was back among mankind. It was roughly at this time that I spotted my first ship, to starboard. A well-lit ship, a big shrimper. I hailed her by radio in several languages but she didn't reply.

My entry into Mar del Plata harbor was somewhat tricky. A sand bar, several miles long, lay across the entrance, and as I was arriving at night I had to be extremely cautious. Nor did I have a detailed chart of this coastline, and the beacons left something to be desired. I got as many indications as I could via radio, so I managed to make my own sketch, showing the different channels. I made it, in part thanks to the weather, which had turned calm and clear. And by going slowly I reduced the risk of running straight onto the sand bar.

Once I was over the bar there was a launch waiting to guide me into the harbor where I could take up my mooring. Once again I was not allowed to step on land, according to the official regulations regarding circumnavigations.

Poulain was all alone in the middle of a huge empty basin of the shipping harbor, across from the Club Nautico, moored to a

white buoy which had been specially re-
painted for me. That was very nice ... I felt
like I was in quarantine. I could hear the
barking of the sea lions on land as they
squabbled at the end of a stone pier. There
was an entire colony of the enormous beasts,
huge seals with manes, the pride and em-
blem of Mar del Plata. From the other side
of the port came a strong odor, from the
hundreds of red and yellow fishing boats.
Hardly a pleasant smell, the stink of very ripe
fish. In the background were old warehouses
bleeding with rust, derelict canneries, and the
night lit up by searchlights. The air was cool;
it was the end of the southern summer.

Usually, when you arrive somewhere by
boat you get off to visit others, they don't
come and visit you. But in this case the
landsmen came to me, and there was something unreal about it. For two months I had
lived in absolute solitude and suddenly it
was rush-hour on board *Poulain*—people
climbing on deck, wandering around, saying
hello. I responded—I hadn't quite forgotten
that you say hello to people—but I didn't
really see them. I was elsewhere. That evening someone brought food, two pounds of

meat, which I devoured as if it were petits fours. In the main cabin were Jean Castel, Christian Bex, my wife Caroline, Didier Ragot, Yves Pouillaude...They were at home in my environment, moving about, but to me they were like spirits. I was sitting at my usual place at the chart table and yet there they were, where usually there was no one. And I knew for a fact that I was still on board, still racing against the record. I was very glad to see them, these are people I care for, family, friends, crew. They were not chance acquaintances, casual encounters, nor were they journalists or hangers-on. But I found it difficult to be on the same wavelength, and conversation faltered. They asked me questions; I answered only after a long pause, as if it were difficult to establish contact, or that the communication had to transit via satellite.

I'd never in my life known visits such as these, not meant to last. We wouldn't be going out and getting drunk together; they had come into a setting which they would soon be leaving, yet I would not. They were like apparitions.

After months of talking to myself alone I

now had the opportunity to share my experience in the Roaring Forties. I could see by the way they looked at me that I sounded like a military officer at a post-battle debriefing, but sensed that they understood what I had been through.

As he came down the companionway Christian noticed the three names I had inscribed above the instrument panel: Chichester, Colas, and Vietnam. Those names had not been there at my departure; I'd scratched them in at some point in the Southern Ocean, to take heart and keep from getting discouraged. Chichester: already an old man, he had sailed around the world, alone, and at a time when very few people had dared to try such a thing. Colas: he had also sailed around the world, although it took him longer, on a boat which I knew; and he was a good man, lost during a race. Vietnam: a war I did not fight; a lot of guys did, against their will.

Those three names offset anything I had to fear. What did I have to complain about, really: I might have been at war with the Southern Ocean, but at least I wasn't being shot at. There's nothing worse than being

sent off to fight when you're twenty—to see
your friends get shot down, get yourself shot
down—all for some bloody war that you
haven't chosen. A member of my family went
through the war in Vietnam as a photographer for an American agency. But I didn't want
to go—at that time I too was a photographer—
because I was afraid of ending up in the
midst of the worst sort of wartime debauchery. I knew, by the time I was 23 or 24, that
the violence of it could captivate, fascinate
me. I got away by the skin of my teeth.

The sea is an inhospitable innkeeper:
you take with you who you are and you live
with that. The sea has a marvelous gift of
revealing the identity of each individual without contributing anything of its own. To
convince myself that what I was going
through could have been a lot worse, I had
etched those three names as points of refer-
ence. The names, though evocative of death,
had no morbid urgency about them—on the
contrary. We must use death in order to live.
We must use the death of loved ones to try
to make our lives better, less pointless. Life
would be vanity were it not permeated with
the idea of death. But to live life to the

fullest does not mean letting oneself go in some existential debauchery. To make the most of life you have to keep your standards, awareness, dignity. Never complain as long as life is on your side. Life is the only thing no man can buy, in any shop.

I used to live near the American Hospital in Neuilly and I remember when Onassis died there. I had a lot of problems at the time, and was desperately broke. But from the moment he died I was richer than he could ever be, despite his fortune, because I had what he could no longer buy. I think the essence and the joy of life are to be found through realizations like this, yet our concept of a civilization of leisure has perverted our ability to understand this: as if life could be carved up into slices, one slice work and one slice pleasure. All of life is pleasure, with powerful moments which one hardly has time to grasp, and moments of routine, and moments where life is difficult and time seems to flow much more slowly.

IT TOOK 48 HOURS to get the boat back in shape. The rigging was inspected and tuned, a new generator was installed, and above all the floats were pumped dry. I knew I had shipped water but I had no idea how much. I asked for an electric pump; it exploded after one minute and I soon gave up the idea of pumping. Didier took my place and from one of the floats he pumped 150 gallons forward, 75 amidships and 75 aft. *Poulain* lost over a ton of water in this way, but we had a lot of trouble finding the leak. The combination of speed and pressure would be enough for a mere pinhead to fill up the float. We would have had to haul her out, cover the floats with soapy water, and inject compressed air into them to find out where the leak was coming from—but of course I didn't have time to do that.

The weather forecast was for a major anticyclonic system in the Atlantic, so I would be headed north in calm conditions. With little speed my float would not fill up so quickly. So I would carry on without getting the leak sealed.

I left Mar del Plata on April 1 with the feeling that my circumnavigation was nearly over and that I was on my way home. The passage from the South to the North Atlantic is not particularly interesting; no longer an adventure, merely travel.

I set off in calm conditions. I raised the sail while still at anchor before heading out to sea; the launch which was vaguely acting as pilot had no need to pull me. On board were Didier, Yves, and the entire crew from Argentina. I had never in my life received such a welcome as in Mar del Plata. The Argentines stayed on board day and night. One of them scrubbed the deck from stem to stern; another did the dishes. The boat had never been so clean and, at the same time, they knew how to remain discreet and very well-mannered. I came away with a warm memory of these people who were Yacht Club members—at least four or five of them on board—and who didn't have a yacht club mentality. They were real sailors, seafarers. They were there to help, not to give stupid advice or admire other people's work. When they left the boat we exchanged warm farewells.

For two days I had trouble getting away from the coast: no wind. I couldn't have been doing more than five knots, maximum. The third day I picked up some wind, then wham, dead calm, the Doldrums. Not just a little calm, but a real glue-pot calm, moving along at the same speed, dragging rain behind it. I'd had virtually no rain during this circumnavigation, except for two days of tropical storms on my north-south run...

And then I noticed, when tacking, that the port shroud had several broken strands. The rigging had been completely inspected in Mar del Plata, and here I found, five days out, that five strands had snapped on the steel cable. If I'd seen it at Mar del Plata I would have changed it, but there had been no sign that it was beginning to give. This was really a pain in the butt, particularly as there was no wind nor wave to speak of. It gave me a chill down my spine. I would have to be bloody careful. I could see *Poulain* had been through a lot and would now show new signs of strain, even on the standing rigging, where you wouldn't have expected such wear and tear in calm weather, and yet...

I was torn between rage at not having any wind and the resignation of saying to myself that it must be a blessing in disguise. The gooseneck, a piece of stainless steel, roughly one and a half inches thick and an inch long, was developing a crack; I had to drill a hole to stop the crack from spreading. The boat was falling apart at the seams; and at the equator I'd be running into a zone of widespread turbulence, with enormous storms over the Amazon. There was the risk of even more pounding for *Poulain*.

But for the moment, bogged down as I was, there was little strain on the boat. Every day Claude Fons would promise me change in the weather but I could see nothing coming. It was as if all the changes I'd been promised had vanished into thin air.

Often as we spoke over the radio I would say, "There's a swell from due north," and Claude would answer, "Impossible, you can't be getting that swell." And yet I was. Nobody knows very well what goes on in this region.

Faint consolation: When it is calm the sailor has a much better view than when it is rough, where each wave is like a hillock and can hide an animal or something like that. And what did I see in that damned calm? A gigantic fin, sticking at least three feet out of the water. I'd never seen such a huge shark. He'd better not start nibbling on my floats! You never knew with these beasts... I don't like them. I don't bother them but I don't like them; let everyone keep to their own territory. One day, shortly after the release of the film "Orca," I heard a woman on the radio who was an expert on killer whales, based in Antibes. She was writing her thesis about them, but she'd never seen one close up. She said that if these whales were dangerous it was because man had bad intentions towards the whale; all animals were basically good, etc. When you know how many sailors have been attacked by sharks when they had plenty of better things to do than to go around bothering them, this kind of Rousseauistic sentimentalism regarding animals is plain criminal stupidity. We believe that animals living in the wild are intrinsically good; but animals are intrinsically wild, that's something different. When we enter their domain they have a choice between two reactions: to flee or to attack. That's it. If you want to be scientific you have to start with that basic premise.

As for my enormous shark, well, I could understand that it would feel before anything else a certain hostility towards me, because the shape of the boat must disturb and frighten it. The boat was totally foreign to the shark's natural habitat—such a stranger that the shark could have chosen his second natural reaction. That's why I would gladly have done without its frightening company.

O N APRIL 14 I crossed the equator. I was only 2800 miles from Brest; but *Poulain* was hardly moving, if at all. Normally—I insist, *normally*—I should have picked up the east-southeasterly trades just before the equator. Not a thing! I had the genoa up the whole time, except when it was too calm: then I was tacking so frequently that I preferred to drop the foresail. I found it bloody boring to keep making these small tacks; their sole purpose was to try to find even a whisper of wind. Slick calm—flat, motionless, infuriating calm. Every day I imagined that it would change, but then I looked at the barometer and found that the atmospheric pressure had not budged an nth of an inch. Nor was Claude's news good at that point. He got his information from satellite-photos: good for an overall forecast but insufficient for precise, local forecasting. Certain weather patterns can develop under the cloud covering filmed by the satellite; they are therefore not taken into account. Claude's forecasts— and this was not his fault—tended to be like those of a television weatherman. And yet he wanted so badly to give me the news I wanted to hear—any action on the weather chart and he would get excited and give me hope. But nothing happened. Every day we had this imbecilic discussion where we would invent a decent weather forecast when there was obviously no decent weather. Meanwhile I was putting in daily runs of 100 or 110 miles.

I had set myself an hourly average of nine knots for my final passage, but I was well below that average. Fine, sunny weather was my lot, and at night the ocean reflected the stars on a sparkling tablecloth of undying calm. It was very beautiful. There was something of a summer holiday in it, and I let myself go to its charm, but I also knew moments of utter dejection as I saw all my work dwindling to nothing. One day I was so fed up that I opened the only bottle of strong liquor I had brought on board, a bottle of rum. I was such a nervous wreck that I could no longer recite Kipling: "If you can... watch the things you gave your life to, broken... you'll be a Man, my son!" Instead I proclaimed: "I'll be a man with a fine shot of rum in his gut." I dithered for a whole week before opening the damned bottle but one evening I broke down and gave it my undivided attention. Perhaps it would make me so paralytic that I'd be able to get my health back. I hadn't been able to sleep a wink, I'd been so obsessed with gaining even one yard of headway, trying all sorts of maneuvers.

It happened to be a Saturday evening that I decided to get drunk, as if to show my solidarity with all the poor wretches whose lives are so full of misery that the only decent thing they have left on a Saturday evening is to get drunk. As I was not used to drinking alcohol (I'd been drinking only water since my departure, except for the little glass of Bordeaux on New Year's Eve), a glass of rum was enough to completely wipe me out.

I had not yet got to the point of thinking that I might not beat the record... Even at three knots I felt sure I'd make it. Still, there was no sport in this sailing drudgery. My mainsail was practically new; the boat was in great shape as far as her ability to catch the wind and move was concerned; and she had never been so light, as three quarters of the food and fuel had already been used up. I had tossed overboard every-thing that had become useless. So she was, potentially, faster than she'd ever been. As soon as I got some breeze she took off. But there was so little—just a few hours a day, and then only in intermittent bursts.

I tried to suppress my anger by reason-ing with myself: I was already lucky to have got that far, homeward bound, in such an uncertain venture. I might be suffering from dead calm, but I could have died in the Roaring Forties, and there was no question which was the lesser of the two evils. So I ordered myself not to complain—in any case what good could it do? I managed to calm my nerves, pressing my hands on the table, taking deep breaths and concentrating, to drive out my rage.

On April 26 I finally reached the vicinity of the Azores. A Breguet Atlantique flew overhead to pinpoint my position. And to greet me. Seen from the sky *Poulain* must have been a sad sight: the anticyclone was stubbornly following me north and the boat was barely moving, her sails hanging limply. I was 1000 miles from home. With typical weather the boat could do it in two or two and a half days; but how long would it take me under these unbelievable conditions?

The Breguet crew told me they'd be dropping me some food. It was quite an experience, watching them maneuver, getting ready to drop their bomb. The package fell 500 yards from the boat. It took me five or six minutes to sail that distance; it kept me busy at least. At the time it was wonderful to open the container and find cutlets, tomatoes, cheese, bread, bananas. What a change from canned food—I was really getting sick of it. But I was so tense that I could no longer eat properly. I had spells where I threw up. I still couldn't sleep, because I knew that I could fall asleep at the very moment when a little breeze came along and miss my chance of getting out of the calm. In a race like the one from La Rochelle to New Orleans I had seen boats which had been neck and neck through the anticyclone of the Azores, only to arrive in New Orleans a week apart. That is why I could not sleep and I was so nervous. I was so shattered, so tired, that I gave in and had my first real coffee—the first stimulant since my departure— while I sailed past the Azores. I'd held off up to then, even at the worst point of the storm in the Forties, because I did not know how often I'd have to call upon my reserves. But with only 1000 miles left to go I could give in to stimulants. They would help me to stay twenty hours a day at the wheel as I tried to make headway. The weather report continued to get it all wrong. Everyone said the anticyclone would eventually move away; sure it did, in the same direction as me. Right on my path—an anticyclone with a homing device.

You dream of finishing a circumnavigation in glory, with a good breeze as you cross the finish line. But not only did I have no breeze—the fog closed in. As I drew near the shipping lane of Ouessant the visibility was 100 feet. And whenever the fog parted briefly it was utter chaos—cargo ships in every direction. Fortunately none of them were going fast. A Chinese ship passed 200 yards from me, in slow motion. Everyone crawled along, watching carefully. So much the better. Because at any moment a cargo ship could slice us in two and destroy my beautiful dream of a race, so close to reaching my goal. I could do nothing but keep watch on the radar; hardly reassuring, the radar confirmed that I was far too well accompanied.

Military planes on maneuver circled overhead. They were there for my benefit, making chandelles and performing circus acrobatics. It kept me entertained. Not long afterwards I received a telegram from Admiral Lefèvre, the maritime prefect, a man after my own heart. I'd been friends with him long before this circumnavigation. He is a cultured, vigorous man, who loves his work. Too often with military men rank erodes their subtlety of spirit, and the moment everyone begins to obey without raising an eyebrow they become prisoners of an infernal psychological gridlock. As obedience is the very foundation of military life it is hard not to become alienated. The higher the rank the greater the tendency towards isolated pride and the belief that everything you say is wonderful because your subordinates are bound to reply "Yes, sir." Lefèvre is one of those who has never fallen into this trap. He is very open, both a man of his times and a gentleman in the old-fashioned sense. He has spent his entire life devoted to his profession and has reached the highest rank of the field he chose when he was twenty. A fine career. So, that he should send me a telegram is a great honor. And he called me "Admiral" as well, and congratulated me: "Quite an exploit!" So I was cited in dispatches of the Navy! Sound the bugle!

25

"**W**HEN WILL YOU get here?" I heard this insistent refrain over the radio several times that day when I was roughly no farther than 120 miles from Brest. I'd get there when I got there! It was not up to me to decide—it was up to the wind. I'd been trying everything for 124 days to get there.

At one point I was so fed up I didn't want to speak to anyone. I switched off the VHF. But at nightfall on May 2, while I was below, I heard three blasts of a foghorn. I went up on deck and 50 yards astern I recognized Jean Bulot on his oceangoing tugboat, *L'Abeille Flandre*. He was a friend, so I switched on the VHF to call him. I thought he had just come out to work on the shipping lane and taken the opportunity to say hello. He told me that, on the contrary, he was there just for me, along with a minesweeper and instructions to protect me as I went through the shipping lane, and to pilot me to the finish line. Bulot asked if I wanted anything. A full dinner, I replied. They launched an inflatable and brought steak and french fries. Jean's a great friend. His job—towing, rescue work—is one of a Lord of the Sea. He picked me up once when I was in trouble off Brest. Jean and his crew reign supreme when it comes to finding their way through anything.

After I had gobbled down my steak and fries I looked to my course again and left the VHF switched on. If Jean spotted any danger he would let me know. He stayed right behind me and adjusted his speed to keep pace with mine. He also passed on a lot of information: the current was moving at such and such, my speed was such and such ... It saved me from having to take my pencil to my chart. This was plotting for a pampered child. So I relaxed, especially as I knew it was my last night at sea. I could smell the land—the thick, moist odor of good Breton soil—something I had not smelled for four months.

Sailors are very sensitive to smells. After several months at sea you suddenly discover ways of perceiving your world that you never use in town. As a rule, the ocean intensifies all your physiological senses. In town you rarely have to see farther than 100 feet; you only focus on what's close to you—a wall, a shop window, a tree, a person. At sea you zero in on what's close to the boat, but you also acquire keen vision for the far horizon.

Living alone re-awakens some of our dormant instincts: the notion of territory, the feeling of presence. On certain atolls the Polynesians were once able to announce: "The schooner will be here tomorrow," before radio communication ever existed; they had no way of knowing, technically, that the schooner was on its way. And yet there it would be, the very next day, with its expected cargo: it had come into their circle, they had felt its presence. I don't think there's anything particularly extraordinary about such a faculty. There's no miracle intuition involved, just human potential, of the kind that, for the most part, is left unused in our modern world because we do not feel the need—or do not want to feel the need—to use it. At the risk of provoking, I would even go one step further and suggest that we know everything which will happen in our lifetime, but we do not wish to take it into account. We hide away our faculties because we voluntarily neglect to use our intellect to the full. It's remarkable to see how, if we're deeply interested in something, we become real experts in that subject. Those who spend their lives with their eyes glued to the stock exchange screen can project: "Hey, the Dow Jones is going to lose three points tomorrow," because both their senses and their understanding have enabled them to anticipate. The same thing happens out at sea; that's why sailing is so exciting. It's not a return from civilization to nature but the rediscovery of another nature; it's finding an ability to survive in the different biological and organic worlds you might encounter in a lifetime. There is a wealth of experience in the wilderness when you throw out all the urgency, all the priorities of life in society. Everyone talks about the frenetic rhythm of modern life—because we take very little time to think about our lives. Instead, the chit-chat of society takes up all our attention. And it doesn't deserve to. On a boat you spend months without listening to the news or opening a paper. When you get home you realize there's nothing more like the newspaper you left with than the newspaper you come home to. The same froth of headlines, the same speeches. Anything out of the ordinary is a miracle, and miracles are few and far between.

A real miracle for me would have been a sudden strong wind, at last. But it was not to be. At one point I even felt we were moving backwards. Despite the launches which had pulled alongside and were following me my last night seemed very long. I was so close to my goal, but until I crossed the line my circumnavigation meant nothing.

By daybreak I realized I had quite a few boats around me—seven or eight launches, very near. I was glad of their presence, but at the same time I was worried that for one reason or another one of them might make a clumsy maneuver and bash into me. One chance in a million, but...

A pale sun came out, but the fog continued to hide Brest. I tacked towards Camaret and found myself, all of a sudden, in the thick of it. Impossible to count all the boats. Among them I could just make out Admiral Lefèvre's launch. The Admiral was in full dress uniform—and he came out for me!

There were a lot of people I did not know, but I had no time for them. I was trying to catch the flood tide to reach the finish line sooner. If I failed to make the most of the current I could be stuck there for another seven or eight hours. At best I still had three or four hours left in the race, and I was in no mood to lose even three feet of ground.

At 7:30 A.M. the fog finally lifted and the bay of Brest lay before me, resplendent with color. The water was sky-blue, intensely blue, criss-crossed with fireboats, all heading towards me. When I crossed the line I thought, "It can all go to hell now; it's of no matter. I've come full circle." A launch pulled alongside and Didier clambered on board. It was a strong, moving moment. We looked each other deep in the eyes and saw it all again, the entire film in fast-forward, from the time of my leaving Brest. Didier had been the last to go ashore . . .

Next to arrive were Caroline and Arthur, his arms filled with a huge stuffed animal; then *Poulain's* designer, then Brincourt. And I began to look around me, seeing with different eyes: boats, noise, celebration, airplanes, helicopters, the submarine *Redoutable*! They all kept a respectful distance, so we had the time to ourselves.

My tugboat was from the port of Brest. I was used to working with her crew, year-round. On the quay was a huge crowd; I felt nervous with so many people watching me, but I found a way round it: I sent one of my crew to the wheel. Let everyone look at him! And I went to hide behind the mast with Caroline and Arthur. A pretty primitive re-action, I admit, since this crowd was very friendly. It was eight o'clock in the morning and some people had been waiting since dawn; they'd gotten up very early, some of them in the middle of the night, and for them the occasion was as thrilling as for me. I had been there when Philippe Monnet returned and was one of the first to go on board. It had been a moving experience, because there's nothing innocent about a boat which reaches its home port after sailing around the world; it's a deadly serious event, emotional in the extreme. A circumnavigation implies something round, complete, conclusive; magical.

I sincerely did not expect there to be such a turnout. I hadn't even imagined that there would be a party. After the ballet of the fireboats the orchestra of the Marine Nationale started up a very jazzy version of *La Mer*. After four months of absolute solitude here I was thrown into a three-ring circus! I found it difficult to get used to the idea.

Then the reporters—radio, television; then the ceremony at the Town Hall... by two in the afternoon I managed to get away with Didier and we made straight for our usual bistro, the *Pré-Vert*, to have a quiet lunch alone. Lunch was the only break in the day; immediately afterwards the infernal rhythm picked up again: radio, television; France Info and France Inter had been tracking my circumnavigation on a day-by-day basis, like a television series...

After four months of total solitude in the world of nature I was once again at the mercy of the world of man.

26

I SPENT MY FIRST NIGHT back on land in the same hotel where I had stayed just before departure: the Oceania. While still out on the ocean I had received a telex signed by the personnel and the management saying that I had been their guest before leaving and that they would like me to be their guest again upon my return. They knew I had financial problems and their offer was disinterested. They wanted to please me. Caroline and Arthur and I had spent Christmas there, a somewhat subdued Christmas, because I was going away to sea . . .

I was happy to find I felt at home at the Oceania; it was as if I were starting my trip again, backwards. My first night on land I couldn't sleep more than two or three hours. I couldn't help visiting *Poulain*. I needed to see what she looked like; I hadn't seen her from the outside for so long. My boat—we couldn't just part like that. There was a solidarity between us. Together we had managed to do that extraordinary thing, to sail around the world.

Life can present us with all kinds of opportunities, but it's rare that it gives us a project we really care so much about. To be able to make it through so many trials, struggling relentlessly, and come through it fulfilled...

The effort will not have been in vain.

EPILOGUE

RACE ORGANIZERS have never imagined sending off a fleet of multihulls on a singlehanded race around the world. Only a few individual sailors—Colas, on *Manureva*, Philippe Monnet on *Kriter*, and myself on *Poulain*—have set off alone, racing against the clock to set the fastest record for a solo circumnavigation.

Multihulls have been around for twenty years now, and I've always thought that if our profession still has a hurdle to overcome it is to enable these boats to take on the Southern Ocean. That is the challenge which, for years, has caused my heart to race and my spirit to soar.

Modern trimarans are light, fast, brilliant. They have made sailing into a swift, gliding sport. The speed, however, can easily turn into a nightmare. In certain types of seas trimarans are potentially very unstable, and the slightest error at the helm can cause an immediate capsize. If there is no one nearby to pick you up, you won't survive beyond ten days...

Because of the speed at which these boats can travel, the strain put on their construction is increased tenfold. A multihull wears out much more quickly than a monohull. Moreover a monohull can withstand windspeeds of up to 100 knots or more, and will handle the weather without too much difficulty. On a multihull, however, wind above 70 knots is a fearful enemy to the boat. It is unadvisable to sail too far to the south, should a strong depression suddenly arise and make it difficult to head north again if necessary.

These parameters obliged both Monnet and myself to sail between latitude 40° and 45° south in the Indian Ocean and between 45° and 57° south in the Pacific. This is much farther north than the usual short route, which hugs Antarctica. In case you hadn't realized, the farther south you sail, the closer you are to the pole and the less distance you have to cover to circumnavigate. On the pole itself all you have to do to circumnavigate is twirl on your feet...

The route I followed was roughly 3800 miles longer than that sailed by the fleet of the Vendée Globe Challenge. I hoped to compensate for that handicap with the boat's potential for speed, and the possibility of daily runs of more than 400 miles. In fact, after a very quick passage from Brest to Cape Horn it was the northward journey from Cape Horn to Brest that took place in the worst conditions of calm I have ever encountered.

The sailors of the Globe Challenge had exceptionally good conditions one year later on the same route. Strong winds never left them, all the way round the globe. Of course the winners all got knocked down, several times, mast in the water. But the advantage of the monohull is that it can right itself, even when rolled right over. A huge multihull like *Poulain* cannot right itself once it has flipped over.

To sail a 75-foot trimaran around the world singlehanded is a wonderful adventure, both of the sea and of solitude. I've never known anything finer.

But life goes on and other challenges await... Now, as I'm finishing this book, I've begun preparation for the next Route du Rhum. It's the finest of all the singlehanded races. I know I'll be in the running and my heart is already beating faster. My boat's called *Esso Super Plus*. We're on our way...

Hotel Miramar. Le Crouesty
January 28, 1990

Other Sheridan House titles of interest

The Third Time Around - The BOC Challenge 1990-91,
  Tony Fairchild
The official account of the world's most challenging yacht race.
Illustrated throughout, *The Third Time Around* is the absorbing
story of the third BOC Challenge, the gruelling 27,000-mile
singlehanded round-the-world yacht race. The Challenge at-
tracts yachtsmen from all over the world to pit themselves and
their craft against each other, the elements, and some of the
world's most hostile seas. The BOC Challenge 1990-91 was
won by a Frenchman, Christophe Auguin.

Effective Skippering - A Comprehensive Guide to Yacht
  Mastery, John Myatt
A complete manual for yacht owners covering every aspect of
yacht management. The book is a distillation of knowledge
gained through practical experience, and explores the reasons
why things on board happen the way they do. Packed with
practical tips and sensible ideas, it will save the reader both
money and trouble.

Single-handed Sailing, Frank Mulville
If you are thinking of making a singlehanded passage, this is
the book to consult, Frank Mulville the man to give you advice
on how to choose your self-steering, adapt rigging and gear,
what supplies to take, how to prepare for bad weather, and how
to keep fit on an ocean passage. "This delightful volume is filled
with dry wit and well-crafted arguments in favor of 'the drug of
solitude.'" *Southern Boating*

By Way of the Wind, Jim Moore
"The best sailboat cruising book to come out in a long time is
Jim Moore's *By Way of the Wind*, an account of his four-year
circumnavigation with wife Molly in *Swan*, the 36-footer he
built with his own hands. Moore's book has a wonderful,
understated tone and his adventures are easy to follow and
appreciate." *Washington Post*